ELLIOTT D. LANDAU
TODAY'S FAMILY

Published by Deseret Book Company, Salt Lake City, Utah
1974

© Copyright 1974 by
Deseret Book Company

Library of Congress Catalog Card No. 74-28592
ISBN 0-87747-543-1

**Printed in the
United States of America
by Deseret Press**

Preface

My column "Today's Family" initially began two years ago in the *Deseret News* with the statement that "the family is alive and well and destined to continue." This was in spite of a very vocal nationwide clamor that the family had been eclipsed by successes attributed to communal living and horrendous divorce statistics. Today I am still of the same opinion: the family is alive and well; in fact, I know of no reputable evidence that refutes the idea that, as Margaret Mead put it, "as the family goes, so goes the nation." In every country that has attempted to substitute "big brother" for the family, there has been revulsion by the people and a return to strengthening the family rather than bagging it.

A recent column in the *National Observer* (July 27, 1974) indicated that thousands upon thousands of people have decided not to marry, but rather to live together and raise a family that way. A close scrutiny of the interviews of both the men and the women involved in these family-like arrangements seems to me to indicate rather clearly that the concept of family is one that is not man-made or contrived.

It appears to me to be a concept that predates man's tinkering with his environment. The attempt to redesign the concept through young adults' simply agreeing to live together is doomed to failure. The words may appear harsh, but it is a fact that in 1973 New York City's Family Counseling Service, for the first time in its history, counseled over three hundred *unmarried* couples. The fraternal arrangement between a man and a woman to live together may proceed normally, although the evidence is that husband-wife strife persists in such arrangements despite the fact that "a little piece of paper" may not officially bind them together.

While obviously not condoning this arrangement, and in fact condemning it, I do believe it is possible to live together without benefit of clergy. However, in my opinion, most of this kind of living merely represents existence on the sexual side only. Remember the song that says "it takes two to tango." In fact, it takes more than two to tango, and it takes more than just a man and a woman living it up to make a family. According to the *National Observer,* many of the couples who have been living together without benefit of clergy had second thoughts about the time their first child was conceived, and certainly second and third thoughts while the child was yet young. Why? Biologically, one can be a father or a mother. The reason for second and third thoughts is simply because it becomes quite obvious that a child brought up by people who are only temporarily committed to one another cannot grow in reasonable family soil. It's difficult enough when the people are committed to one another, even irrevocably. It takes work to make the marriage contract work. When there is nothing binding a couple but a verbal agreement based upon sexual and intellectual compatibility, that tenuousness of commitment permeates the life-style of the couple.

The second reason the agreement to live together doesn't work is because when the first baby comes along the facts are very clear—when dad decides he's had enough of this makeshift arrangement, he just gets his things together and says, "Well, baby, it just didn't work, did it." With this, he sallies forth into the world, ready to bring his sterling qualities to bear upon another unsuspecting female. And whom does he leave home holding the baby? You guessed it. He leaves a young woman who is the mother of his child with no one to support her, no one to share with her, no one who cares. And so if she's lucky she will take up with some other "with it" young man who has just left his last companion. How long will he stay with lady number 2?

Since the male traditionally splits* the family, leaving the situation just described, it seems to me that the women of America need to reaffirm an insistence upon certain equality. Why should mother (biological, to be sure) be left with baby? And how often do you think the splitting father lovingly and tenderly takes his issuance with him? Once again, the overwhelming preponderance of evidence tells us that he rarely says to himself, "This is my beloved child, too." Indeed, he has sowed his seeds, and without waiting for the harvest, he leaves his plow and bids the fair lady adieu.

Of course the family is in trouble. It always has been, and it always will be. But that's the fun of it. That's the joy

---

*In the sense that he (a) moves out physically and (b) seems not to feel as bound as does his "wife."

of it. That's the experience of it. No man has been promised a primrose path.

Quite frankly, I am at a loss to understand the reasoning that says that if two people do not marry formally, there is less likelihood of trouble between them. There is no evidence whatever that the mere agreement to live together produces less tension and less trouble. If the commitment is real, then the decision to make it legal or to bind it in heaven is a perfectly legitimate one. A family grounded in a firm civil and religious commitment is more likely to withstand the vicissitudes of family strain.

Today's Family is my minor attempt to focus the light of introspection upon the variety of problems and joys that highlight the family experience. When a couple agree to agree that living together will be an adventure or an experiment in mutual sharing and decision making, then the cement necessary to create a good family is well on its way to being set. The decision to make a relationship temporary from the first seems to forecast the tentativeness of the arrangement.

One of the primary considerations of this book is that the life of the child is as important as, if not more important than, the individual contentment of either or both of the parents. The purpose of the family is to lay the groundwork for the healthy growth of the next family to follow—that is, the family that will develop from the children born into the original family. I am unable to conceive of a philosophy that says that marriage is simply a therapeutic arrangement for a male and female who commit themselves intellectually, physically, and emotionally to one another alone.

May I suggest the wisdom of a husband and wife reading the book together and making it the focal point for frequent discussions. Experience has also taught that children from the age of accountability onward profit much from their input to the content wherever it is relevant. The family experience of family reading and family discussion provides additional climate for intrafamily communication.

Acknowledgments

Perhaps the greatest acknowledgment one can give would be to say that he gives thanks for growing up in a good family where the father and mother were Herman and Bertha Landau. The epilogue to this book tells more about my parents.

I should like to acknowledge the contributions of thousands of University of Utah students who have shared with me their experiences of family over a twenty-year period.

I came to Utah in 1955; now twenty years later I am wiser, and, of course, older and not anywhere near the person I was when first I knocked. For the few short years that I lived with Shirley Kaplan Landau, my first wife, who died in an accident on June 11, 1957, and who left me with two babies, now 20 and 18, I give my eternal thanks for a good start in family life. I should like to acknowledge the woman who so very bravely took over this family and added two more children to it—Zona Stewart Landau, my wife since 1958. Hers is a saga of courage and repeated attempts to make a family out of what was once a shambles, disillusion, and heartbreak. We are both proud of the fact that we have persevered in the face of nearly insurmountable odds. We candidly agree that the family is the greatest and the most difficult institution to maintain with harmony, peace, and love. Those moments when we have achieved all of these are cherished. Even the moments during the process that were not happy, that were full of fear, even terror, disappointment, and marital strife, are deeply appreciated by both of us. We both acknowledge a force greater than ourselves, greater than all other human beings that have ever lived upon the earth, as being a binding one.

I acknowledge my deep and abiding friendship with Harold B. Lee, the late president of The Church of Jesus Christ of Latter-day Saints. In the intimate hours that we spent together, I learned at his feet.

I should like to acknowledge all of the people who worked visibly and invisibly in the *Deseret News* Living Section, where these articles first appeared over a period of nearly two years. The unceasing labors of Evelyn Mazuran, editor of the Living Section, need to be especially mentioned. I often write in bursts of unbridled enthusiasm, throwing logic and linguistics to the wind. Mrs. Mazuran capably and with candor and kindness takes these ''flaming phrases'' of mine and tempers them with skill and ingenuity.

I particularly wish to acknowledge the editors of the *Deseret News*, on whose pages every one of these articles has previously appeared. It was their faith in this writer and in their readership that has inspired this column to appear each Wednesday in the *Deseret News*. The general manager, William B. Smart, colleague and mentor in this endeavor, is everlastingly acknowledged. My good friend, William James Mortimer, general manager of the Deseret

Book Company, has continually earned my highest regards. The detailed and exacting editing of Eleanor Knowles are also acknowledged.

My thanks for the dedication of Gail Reidling, who patiently keeps accurate account of what I write, when I write it, and then manages to keep neat files for my future reference.

To Keith Eddington and associates, for carefully designing and making mere cold print graphically lovely, I am indebted for this book and for my other books to which he has put his genius. There are three other men who have somewhat silently, yet vigorously impressed me with their family life: Russell M. Nelson, general president of the Sunday School of The Church of Jesus Christ of Latter-day Saints; Joseph B. Wirthlin, first counselor in the Sunday School; and Rick Warner, second counselor. I also acknowledge all of the members of the general board of the Sunday School with whom I serve. Each of them has made an impact upon my life.

The technical contributions of Virginia Satir, Theodore Lidz, Ivan Boszormenyi-Nagy, Robert Friedman, D. D. Jackson, R. D. Laing, and L. C. Wynne are also acknowledged.

Jan Garrett has been a faithful secretary, collator, and willing worker these past two years. To Barbara LaPray and Jean Milligan I owe a final word of thanks for their line-by-line reading, commentary, and assembling of these pages.

THE TAPESTRY

The tapestry	1
The American family—a unique system	4
The peculiar American family	7
Is the family obsolete?	10
The biology of the family	13
What the family means to the child	16
The significance of parental support	19
How the family must evolve	23
The development of parents	27
No substitute for mother	30
Mothercraft	33
Becoming human	36

THE PROBLEMS

The problems	41
Peace at home	45
Be it ever so hollow	48
Family conflict and school behavior	51
School behavior problems and the family	54
Fat kids	57
Obesity in children	61
Who are the "street people"?	65
Drug disease—what's the cure?	70
The families of drug addicts	74
The real danger of marijuana	77
Dead from overdose	80
Happiness without drugs	83

XVII

THE STRENGTHS

The strengths	87
Learning how to communicate	94
The real meaning of parent-child communication	98
Listening with the third ear	101
Touching isn't taboo	104
The family interaction grid	107
Every family needs rules	111
What kept 200 adolescents from trouble?	114
What kind of family discipline?	116
Freedom isn't license	119
In families self-esteem is vital	122
Making good behavior pay	125
Be positive for a change	127
Give praise for kindness	130
Tradition	133
Secret survival in society	136

THE CHILDREN

The children	141
What makes your child tick?	146
Three types of children today	149
The needs of children	152
The earliest years and later learning	155
Helping your child before school starts	158
Competition—does it help or hinder the child?	161
Money and character development	165
Have youngsters changed?	168
The adolescent hassle	172
Young adulthood	176
Sex education for boys	179
Counseling adolescent virginity	183
Lost love	187
Middle class rip-off	190
Religion and revolt	193
An open letter to junior high school teachers	196

THE CHANGES

The changes	201
Interfaith marriages	203
The family and adoption	207
After adoption, what?	210
Change hurts	213
Coping with moving	216
When a little child is dying	219
When a child is dying—a trauma for loved ones	223
Mourning for mates	227
Helping those who mourn	230

EPILOGUE

Reflections on their fiftieth **235**

Index **239**

THE TAPESTRY

The implications of the term "the tapestry of the family" are that the individual members of the family may not be represented merely as entities enclosed in little boxes or in circles (cf. "The Family Interaction Grid" on p. 107). One has only to approach a fine tapestry hanging in the Cloisters in New York City to comprehend the minute structure that is necessary to eventually weave a full-blown character.

While it is true that one may diagram the family rather easily for the purposes of analysis and interaction theory, it is also true that a family is something more than the mere sum of its parts. It would be the height of folly to describe the family as being made up of a mother, a father, and so many children. Upon the matrix of this tapestry is woven and interwoven the variety of personalities that comprise the people in the family. Each of these is a delicate webbing that is not a single dimensional representation of a human being. Imagine, if you will, applying a magnifying glass to a segment of tapestry for the purpose of examining the intricate design. Much like a needlepoint pattern, one sees less than what went into needlepoint when one merely identifies the picture for what it is. Its graphic or literal representation, as true as it may be described, is nonetheless inadequate to fully delineate the complexity of the work that went into it. So, too, families are much like this.

The individual variations within the family are intricate, detailed, and not easily described by simply saying that there are this many males, this many females in the family. In previous volumes I have utilized adult fiction to bring to the consciousness of the reader and student or parent the marvelous intricacy of the tapestry of the developing human beings of parents and of teachers and children. The fictional approach to human growth and development is frequently described as bibliotherapy or literatherapy. The work of Dr. Michael Shiryon, of the Kaiser Institute Department of Psychiatry, in using Yiddish and Hebraic fiction (including many biblical stories) with mental patients in various California hospitals, is especially intriguing.

The family has been variously described in many short stories and novels that stand out. Among these are two novels of great stature. *A Death in the Family*, by James Agee (Grossett & Dunlap, 1970), and *A Mass for the Dead*, by William Gibson (Atheneum, 1968) are especially brilliant in their detailed analyses of the interaction of human personalities within the family structure. For an unforgettable experience, both of these are "must" reading. Both are cited in this brief introduction to this section of the book because they exemplify the writer attempting to tease at the tapestry of the family structure in such a manner as to make unforgettable the complexity, ingenuity, and delicate nuances of intrafamilial responses. Both books illustrate what I have been trying to say—that the family is more than the sum of its parts, more than the simple addition of the sexes within the family, more than knowing who and how many there are; indeed, the family is an embroidery of indescribable human variations that are only touched upon in the chapters that follow in this part of *Today's Family*.

The family, then, is a biological and sociological colloidal emulsion. It is not necessarily an entity, though it may become so in time. It is, like an emulsion, a solution in suspension. It is often blotchy, murky; at times there are patches of clarity. In many ways, much of what the family is cannot be changed. In this respect, the chapter on "The Biology of the Family" may be instructive. The significance of the family in its protective web and cloak originating within the vacuoles of the parents is described in other chapters in this section. As one finishes "The Tapestry of the Family," he should feel that he has a reasonably accurate working definition of the role of the family and the life space of both the parents and their children.

The American family— a unique system

Many aspects of American family life are in trouble; there is no question about that. I do not think this presages the end of the family, but one needs to recognize the vast differences between the American concept of family life and that of most of the rest of the world.

In the first place, most of America is characterized by its rejection of the family. Our own parents and grandparents are not considered models. In fact, in America we consider that one hasn't matured unless he separates from his parents, whereas ninety percent of the world's peoples would never consider leaving the family hearth for a place of their own.

Some years ago a friend of mine, a medical professor, indicated that he was returning to India to help find a husband for his sister. When scoffed at for this ancient practice, he indicated that our system of finding our own mates was far from ideal. After all, in America we marry for love, and two out of four marriages fail; in fact, in some places the figure is closer to three out of four.

In most of the world, children do not have the luxury of self-choice for a life partner, but there is no evidence that this ancient procedure results in less marital happiness. We raise our children proudly in America so that they will become self-reliant and independent. This produces an aggressiveness and precocity that strikes people from other countries immediately.

May I quote from a letter I received from a distinguished young British mother and author who is reporting upon her stay with the family of a fellow American author and family: "A somewhat intimidating family of geniuses—one daughter a brilliant cellist, and I mean brilliant. But there was a reassuringly normal nine-year-old son...."

We pride ourselves on children who excel, who outshine their parents, and we pay the price for this in noisy, articulate, self-centered children.

Next, we raise our children with absolute equality in the family, thus giving nothing to either the eldest or the youngest. Therefore we unconsciously develop intense family rivalry among the children. Our emphasis on the equality of each child begets a mad race for parental favor.

Nowhere in the world is there the prolonged period of adolescence that we suffer through here. It starts at eleven and goes on well into the twenties. Consider this most interesting fact. Adolescence is a ceaseless search for identity and understanding; the young person's attempt to place himself in society; his quest to discover who he is, why he is there, and where he is going. But in most of American society there is no respect for authority or tradition, and so every explanation by the over-thirty world is rejected as irrelevant.

Good? Bad? Neither is probably correct. With no authority models to follow, the young in America lead out to nowhere and toward nothing.

Finally, the American scene is complicated by the fact that nowhere else in the world do our unmarried females have the independence of choice that ours do. Our girls, then, are "the principal architects of their own marriages." This boldness, while unusual, is still a subservient freedom when compared with that of the male. Nonetheless, both sexes in America enjoy unparalleled freedom in mate selection, occupational choice, and life-style.

The American family is a unique institution. It has survived some radical departures from world tradition. To continue to be vital, it will need to reexamine some of its uniqueness and perhaps reject what has been taken for granted.

The peculiar American family

Family life isn't easy. When two people of distinctly different heritages attempt to join forces and rear a family, there is bound to be trouble. So what else is new? Trouble rarely has meant scrapping the product. I emphatically state that the family is not the Edsel Ford.

The American family is forged from a mixture of very complicated factors. Perhaps the most difficult stumbling block to successful families is the fact that, in middle-class America particularly, the once patriarchal male authority has been seriously eroded. TV serials, cartoons, and jokes make persistent fun of the ineffectual American male.

Coupled with this male deficiency is the fact that the assertive power of women in America is stronger than anywhere else. Women, in fact, have the greater share of decision-making authority in this country. They have considerable economic power; they bear most of the responsibility for the moral guidance of the family; and they have great power to break up the family and retain a considerable degree of protection for themselves under the law. But not all is sweetness and light for them. The anxieties of mothering are frightening and legendary. Since most of the child-rearing falls to the mother, it is she who spends sleepless nights wondering where she went wrong.

Finally, in America we grow old as do people nowhere else. In nearly every part of the world growing old brings such rewards as respect, care, and even veneration. In America, however, the beginning of any dependency is the beginning of the end. America celebrates youth and life, while growing old leads to psychological hurts.

For every characteristic I have named here, one may find examples in other cultures, for America is not the only country with these characteristics. For instance, there are assertive women in Communist Russia. But nowhere do all of these characteristics combine into an integrated system; nowhere is there the ceaseless struggle for personal independence. If anything represents a thrust of American society, it is the striving for independence and equality, a drive that dominates all that we do, all that we are.

None of what I have described is in and of itself bad or good. It becomes bad or good only when placed in context. If we wish to prize autonomy, then we must suffer the children who are produced in the system that courts this trait. If we wish to continue the American family, then we must learn to put up with our aggressiveness or change our goals. Changing or moderation of goals is possible within each family. For example, the fact that the American female is the architect of the moral fiber of the home in which she lives is inevitable in the situation where mother is home and dad goes to work each day. In a family where both parents work, it is conceivable that there can be more equal sharing of the responsibility for teaching ethics.

The vital task is for families to decide what it is they want or do not want to have happen and where they want to put the barricades. American family life will never be static, but it will endure and prevail.

Is the family obsolete?

Folks have been holding their heads about family life since biblical days.

Schopenhauer once told the story of two porcupines who found themselves in an awkward situation one bitter winter day. Since they were freezing, they moved closer together to keep warm. They soon found they were hurting each other with their quills, but when they moved apart, they found they were freezing again. They moved together and apart, freezing and hurting, until they found the optimum distance at which they could stay warm and still not hurt each other too much.

A brief survey of recent professional literature concerned with the family in America mostly forecasts the end of the family in its present state. The porcupine analogy seems to sum up the consensus of professional opinion.

Is the family obsolete? Divorce statistics are bloodcurdling. There is little doubt that troubled children come from troubled families. Every fact of modern life seems to be shouting that the family has had it. But has it?

Nearly all totalitarian societies have attempted to obliterate the notion of family, but all have backed away from this, because when alternative arrangements for bringing up children have been tried, they have failed. Both in the Soviet Union and in Red China the people would not tolerate this attempt at dissolution. Too many free-style communes have developed their own kinds of tyranny. It is interesting to note that at one commune when folks were asked to pose for a picture, even though there was shared child-rearing and no marriage, as middle-class America understands it, children ran to their natural parents to pose.

Theodore Lidz, chairman of the Department of Psychiatry at Yale University, says this about the family in his book, *The Person* (Basic Books, 1968): "It is an institution for which no workable substitute has been found except in very special circumstances."

One of the real problems with those who see extended families or no families as being a viable alternative to the present family with all of its problems is the very evident fact that man, unlike other species, needs a protracted period of nurturance to survive. A child needs only one or two very concerned adults in the earliest years. In addition to this lengthy time with adults, he also needs people who consider his welfare as important as or more important than their own.

While it may be true that the conventional family faces problems with a "quiet desperation," it is also true that "families" in new life-style communities simply pack up and disappear when the going gets rough.

Because the family is in trouble doesn't mean it must be scrapped as a way of life. Let me suggest some sensible things all families need to do in order to avoid failure.

The most significant answer I know is for humans who intend to become parents to study something of the needs of children. Every couple needs to learn to dig deeply into their children and themselves so that they reflect genuine authenticity.

We need to know what we truly value, and to teach it with love and dignity to those we birth. A family needs to be a sharing experience, and the success of one must become the joy of all. If we abandon the nuclear family and try to encourage adults to discover only themselves, children will be ignored so that the adults in their family can do their own thing.

The balanced wisdom of true adulthood can make the family work. Every family needs to be extended; we need to extend our concern, extend our hearts, and extend our wishes and dreams. And above all, parents need to believe in the coalition of adults lest the children of the family live in infinite corridors of despair.

The mature family is alive and well and living—and it shall endure.

The biology of the family

It seems to me there are some indisputable biological facts about the family that all need to know. These are not new, nor known only to a few privileged persons. It is information that is so self-evident that no amount of innovation or alteration in the family structure, no political or sociological dogma can have much effect upon it.

The nuclear family is composed of two generations—parents and children—with different needs, responsibilities, and obligations. Whenever there is much deviance from these, the family is in trouble. Should adults deny this and behave as if they belong to the same generation as their children, they may expect that one day their children will treat them as peers, and that day all semblance of discipline and respect will disappear. Children who are allowed to behave as if they belonged to their parents' generation are indulging in behavior inappropriate to their age.

Each parent in marriage needs to realize that he came from a family whose background may be entirely different from his spouse's. As they merge into a new unit, it takes a great deal of intellectual and emotional energy for both to realize that they need to make significant alterations in their interpersonal relationships in order to compensate for these differences. The crucial factor here is, which differences can be set aside and which are indispensable to their continuing good health. Having solved the problem of meeting each other's needs with some reasonable give and take, a couple then merge to form a coalition that takes upon itself the task of rearing children.

The children of a couple receive their primary training in group living within the family, and they remain dependent upon their parents for many more years than do members of any other species. Intense emotional bonds are built between the two generations.

The essential learning that takes place within the family is the knowledge of how to live outside the unit and, even more significant, knowledge of how to develop a family of one's own when the time comes. Thus, if the intensity of emotional attachment within the family is too strong, too erratic, it handicaps the child in acclimatizing to the outside world. (A good example of this is the child who fears school as a separation from his mother, which he cannot bear.)

Thus the expression "love at home" is not incorrect, but it must be love with clear and definable limits regarding the affectional and sexual relationships between both generations.

I have indicated that the generation gap is an important part of the family structure. This does not mean that there ought to be a communication gap. It is entirely possible to have free-flowing communication even though there's a difference of opinion about the length of hair and hemlines.

To sum up:

—Marriage is difficult when two people from entirely different families join. Maturity allows each to give in enough to be comfortable as a new unit.

—Each couple must become a working team so that basic ideals and goals are shared with the children, who look to their parents for direction.

—Each family unit must be sufficiently mature so that it does not hold on to the children to satisfy its own needs.

What the family means to the child

The primary function of the family is to further the integrated development of its children. More simply stated, in order for children to be fully functioning individuals, both as children and later as adults, they need to have their emotions, behavior, and consciences so meshed that they are able to survive the vicissitudes of human existence. Generally speaking, troubled children tend to spring from a degree of family disintegration.

There are three tasks that must be achieved in each family that can either aid or hinder integration: (1) the coalition of the parents, (2) the maintenance of boundary lines between the different generations, and (3) a strong adherence to the gender-linked roles. Each of these indispensable tasks has been subject to a great deal of verification in countless case histories that appear before the social agencies throughout this land. I have seen this documented time and again in counseling situations I have directed, observed, and participated in during the past twenty years.

The word *coalition* is simple. It means that parents, instead of representing competing agencies or individuals in the home, need to be bound up in a common purpose. Too often when the major share of the breadwinning is undertaken by the wife, for whatever good and sensible reasons, the position of family protector is also assumed by the wife, and this is contrary to the development of the healthy family.

This does not imply that a woman should not work, that she should not even earn more than her husband. But her earning powers ought not to take precedence over her natural role—that of satisfying the child's nurturant and emotional needs.

I do not mean that a father cannot be an affectionate person, but when he becomes the person whose responsibility is affectional, then we no longer have a coalition in the marriage, but a dominance.

There is a bit more to the word *coalition*. If either parent is subjugated, threatened, despised, or denigrated by the other spouse, then children grow up with distorted views of that parent as a person. There may, in fact, be a great deal of discord between parents, yet the basic quality of mutual respect can endure. If children are forced to shift their loyalties to either of two parents, even in the case of divorce where this is sort of built into the relationship, then there is no coalition, but polarization.

As to boundary lines between generations: As they grow, children need to separate from their parents. They should not be made to feel responsible for a parent's happiness, as is often the case of children who grow up and in their forties or fifties are still not married. There is a difference between feeling responsible to a parent as a dutiful child, and feeling responsible to one's mother as her only source of happiness.

Children must not become *the* source of happiness for their parents. They may be a source of pleasure, a significant factor in the parent's life, but they must never take the place of life itself. No child can enter into an intimate relationship —marriage—with a person of the opposite sex while still tied to one of his parents, especially the parent of the opposite sex. We do not own our children in any sense. They are not ours except for a very brief span of time.

It is the familial task to raise them so they can leave us comfortably.

As to gender-linked roles: It was once said that "biology is destiny." This is not entirely true, but it isn't too far wrong. There are very clear anatomical differences between men and women. The nonpsychotic mother looks at, holds, and feels toward her child in a different way than does the father. Barring a certain degree of mental ill health in either parent, differing sex roles are fairly evident. When avant-garde couples decide to completely forget sex role identities (if this is at all possible), they run a great risk of producing children who will not develop clear sex role identities.

This does not imply that men should not wash dishes, diaper babies, or share responsibilities. But if, in their zeal to show how "with it" they are, parents reverse sex roles, their children will have severe developmental problems.

The significance of parental support

When Hitler started to saturate-bomb London, it was decided that all children were to be evacuated to the country. Have you ever wondered what the response of the children to wartime conditions is? Since World War II there has hardly been a year without war in some part of the world. And in every war there are children who must, along with their parents, bear the emotional strain of noise, fatigue, death, fire, separation, and loss. How do they survive?

I thought it quite amazing to discover that Anna Freud, who did the most definitive work on children in war in a volume entitled *Young Children in Wartime* (London: Allen and Unwin, 1942), discovered that during the time of the London blitz all children over the age of two had acquired a knowledge of the significance of air raids. They all recognized the sound of airplanes; they all realized that houses would fall when bombed; and they understood fully the significance of taking shelter. They understood their fathers leaving and going off to war.

What did puzzle the children was the reason they had

to be evacuated, since after the raids all was calm and peaceful until the next sound of the siren. Many children felt their mothers should be evacuated also, so that they too could be safe. It was particularly poignant to learn that the children had intense feelings about home, even though they were fully aware that their homes were totally destroyed. All they wanted to do was return, despite the fact that the homes did not exist.

Dr. Freud studied the trauma attached to the loss of home, neighborhood, friends, familiar people, and places. Though the bombing experiences were often severe, she observed that children who had the support of stable parents were able to endure the most severe shock, while children who were separated from their parents, for whatever reason, suffered profoundly from identical experiences.

In the opinion of many students of childhood there is no trauma—not death, not failure in school, not dishonor—that cannot be mastered and even conquered by any child provided he has the support of at least one of his parents, and preferably both of them. Difficulty arises when, in order to cope with the magnitude of the problem, the adults in a child's life turn away from him. They do not realize that parental grief is contagious.

I know of a family in which a young girl had to face a serious back operation. It literally convulsed the family, yet the parents rallied and effected an emotional coalition between them that sustained the child through a year of intense suffering.

A much less serious situation occurs with school failure. I am aware of a teenager who simply seemed to forget for over a year that there was a high school. She showed up nearly every morning and then left class to sit on the school steps or ride through the countryside with a variety of sixteen-year-olds driving vehicles too expensive for their pocketbooks. She came from a home without a father but populated by two good people—a mother and an older teenage brother who were the only support she had, and they weren't giving it. They weren't mean folks; they had just given up trying, and so they made no bones about their withdrawal of support. So what was this unhappy child left with? Nothing but the commiseration of some of her peers who, though they tried, finally threw up their hands and withdrew whatever little support they once provided.

It seems that when folks are the most unloveable is when they need the most love—but they don't get it. When children at any age are faced with failure in any endeavor—dating, sports, friends, disappointment—the only possible way out and up is to feel the support of parents who are stable.

Robert Frost once said, "Home is the place where when you get there they have to take you in."

President David O. McKay said it somewhat differently. He said, "Home is the place where when you get there they *want* to take you in."

When children "blow it," they hurt inside. I have never met any children who enjoyed the failures and disappointments they often face. Ignorance is not bliss. Even so-called stupid children have emotions.

Children do have great inner strengths. They can bounce back from many horrible experiences. Indeed, they do. And when they have adults in their lives who support them in times of stress, they may bounce back with even greater strength than they had before.

Children are not little adults. They are not miniatures. They experience trauma in profound ways. They often cannot ask for help. It hurts too much to do this. Nevertheless, they need adult support volunteered over and over, in spite of the fact that they sometimes reject that support.

How the family must evolve

Infants of the human species spend more years being totally dependent upon their parents than do infants of any other species. It takes nearly three years of almost total control by adults before a human is able to take even the most rudimentary care of himself. During this period, a mother learns how totally dependent the infant is.

For adults who are reasonably emotionally normal, the transition to toddlerhood offers some respite from the endless hours of total attention that must be given to the newborn. However, those few adults who are emotionally immature or for whom life's circumstances have made the child a source of special comfort and companionship, the transition into the preschool years may be especially difficult; the adult has become too accustomed to lavishing attention upon the child.

Family evolution refers to the great importance of parents, especially the mother, becoming aware that the intensity of care demanded by the child at two must be changed as the child grows older. If this evolution of operational behavior does not occur, the procedures of infancy carry over to the preschool years, where they are distinctly inappropriate. Thus, whereas it was perfectly acceptable to keep the child away from street crossings at two, the same type of surveillance at six would only embarrass and humiliate the child.

The mother who cannot adjust to the necessity for changing the magnitude of concern between three and, say, six, finds that she has a rebellious and difficult child on her hands. After all, the process of growing up means that there is a gradual separation from the nuclear unit. The typical triad (mother, father, child) is cracked by the movement of the child toward his appropriate peer group. Thus, the child requires a relaxing of the attention given in earlier years. Parents who, for whatever reason, cannot do this alienate the child, and these parents may be sure that there will be a backlash.

Another dangerous situation that too often exists is the symbiotic relationship that can develop between mother and child. Though it does happen between father and child, it is more typically characteristic of mothers and children of the opposite sex. When there is this symbiotic relationship, the parent is said to derive as much emotional satisfaction from the child as the child does from the parent. Of course, parents must derive satisfaction from their children. Parents would not behave affectionately if they did not receive reciprocal affection from the child. They are reinforced by the child's love and are more likely to repeat the loving behavior.

First children, especially, cause their parents much concern in the realm of feeding. Inexperienced parents often feel that their children will starve if they don't eat exact proportions of food. While it is expected that agitation over food intake in infancy is somewhat legitimate, the same level of concern must not continue as time goes by. It is the one problem in early childhood that ought not to become a locus of concern unless it appears that the child is suffering severe weight loss, dehydration, or in any other way manifests severe or bizarre emotional behavior.

When we talk of family evolution, then, we are really saying that in order for parental responses to change or evolve, parents ought to grow as the children grow.

Here's another example: As an adolescent develops into maturity, there is immediately evident a certain combativeness on his part as he interacts daily with his parents. For instance, whereas at seven or nine he usually accepted the dictums of his parents without much fuss, at fifteen there may develop sharp differences of opinion. It is not that he has become obstinate, ornery, or downright mean; it is just that he has become fifteen.

To expect the same behavior at fifteen over a difference of opinion between father and son that one expected at nine would be to court disaster. After all, the peer group has taken over, and if there is no evolution of expectation on the part of the parents, they will be desperately hurt by what is simply an evolution on the part of the child.

As the child's drive for autonomy increases, it is important that parents understand this movement toward self-actualization. This does not mean that the child needs to get everything he wants or that he can bully his family. It does mean that these frictions, based upon the child's evolution from a dependent organism to a more independent one, need to be appreciated by his parents. Should they be completely unacceptable to them, the arena is set for some battles that are sure to follow.

The development of parents

The notion that parenthood is a time of personal development is an exciting concept. Too often we view parenthood as the end of the line as far as our personal accomplishments are concerned, but parenthood is a dynamic, not static, time of life. For each stage in the growth of children, there is a similar one for parents.

During infancy the great developmental task of parents is to learn to interpret the child's needs. Unconcerned, unintelligent, or immature parents are unable to feel the needs of their children. So, when the baby cries, some parents might hurt him for his "inconsiderateness." During the period of infancy, which means "without speech," the child cannot say what he needs. Thus, parents need to be continually sensitive to the variety and intensity of cries.

In the next stage of the child's life, known as toddlerhood, parents have the task of learning to accept the child's growth and development as being normal and not a deliberate frustration. Too often his ambulatory development at this time means that he will be into everything and will put everything into his mouth. Parents whose own growth and development lag behind their child's during this stage often report bitter resentment and hurt as their baby becomes an exploring rover.

In the fourth and fifth years of life the child, now called a preschooler, often sheds his homelike existence for some sort of preschool experience. At this time he and his parents need to learn to tolerate separation one from another. A parent who has learned to enjoy the total dependence of the child upon him may find the separation disturbing. In fact, the child also needs to learn to tolerate the times he will spend without parents around. If parents have sent messages to the child that *they* need him for *their* comfort, then he is unable to break away easily, and trauma is attached to preschool experiences. It is necessary for them to allow him to assert himself and to show initiative. Yet, it is equally important that they know how to set limits when he needs them. Once again, this is not picked up by parents automatically. It is for them, as well as for the child, a growth process.

During the school years, six through twelve, the child finds that his peer group is very important. In his search for their acceptance, he frequently slights his parents and rejects them in ways that are both overt and subtle. Parents who need continued reassurance of their child's faithfulness are the unhappiest people in the world during this time. The anxiety of separation needs to be overcome by all. The process of child-rearing is a co-development of both children and parents. It is not a one-way street.

Finally, during adolescence, as the child is being moved more and more into the peer realm, he increasingly finds that he doesn't want or need the attention of his parents. If they do not understand this development, they view his rejection of them as a betrayal. Parents need to use this time also to develop themselves, to rebuild their lives with a great degree of independence from their children. Parents, you see, are not just vehicles for the care of children. They are people whose development continues through the birth of their children to their own deaths. Anything less spells disaster for parenthood. Human personality continually develops and does not stop at the end of adolescence.

Viewed this way, parenthood becomes a further development of childhood. It is not fixed, not a plateau. It is a very real time for humans to grow with their children.

No substitute for mother

One definition of a day-care center is "a facility in which certain women who have borne children can unload them on other women—for a price about equal to the mother's earning capacity. A day-care center frees enlightened but fertile females from household drudgery. With it, and no toddlers underfoot, they can overcome sexist prejudice whilst bracing themselves for the pleasures of factory work and office employment." This tidbit is from Bernard Rosenberg's *Dictionary for the Disenchanted* (New York: Regnery, 1972).

Having recently returned from the annual meeting of the American Orthopsychiatric Association in New York, I was struck by this gem of a definition, since some of my time was spent in listening to the inane prattling of people dedicated on the one hand to providing mental-health services for a very distraught America, and on the other to discussing how best to pry apart mothers who wish to enter the lists of the working girls.

These, as I saw them pour out of the New York office buildings, seemed to be continually talking about some fellow or other who might want to settle down to a family. These who are working, at least in New York, seemed to be quite willing to exchange the whole glamour bit for a nice guy who would love them and keep them in a manner to which they were unaccustomed.

I saw plenty of the so-called liberated crazies with their eyes darting about for simple farm boys—boys who believe that there is a great difference between the way most mothers care for their children and the way just anyone unconnected biologically would.

There always have been and there always will be those women temperamentally unsuited to rearing fine families. In fact, with no little persuasion I am sure I can get any mother to indicate that more than once in her child-rearing life she would have exchanged places with anyone from Bedlam.

All this means simply that on any one day any natural mother might be at the end of her rope physically and emotionally. The discussions I participated in seemed not to be looking at temporary insanity during any twenty-four-hour period with children at home, but rather to be declaring flatly that the nuclear family is dead and no one has attended the funeral yet. The corpse is rotting, yet it still manages to lie there despite the fact that everyone but the corpse knows of its demise. Some talks pictured children being reared among groups of people who simply love them. What does it matter, as long as there is love?

L'il Abner once said that love was better than hate because it was more affectionate. I think the matter is not as simple as the ordinary usage of the word *love*. What is this thing called love? Does it mean that the folks who will extend themselves to care for anyone and everyone's children are certified "loving"? Who attests to this?

I would only shudder if there comes a day—and I predict that that day is near at hand—when a certificate, accompanied by a certain degree of formal and on-the-job experience, trumpets that its holder is a bona fide mother substitute for any child.

There was a time when modern child watchers were touting the Israel kibbutz model as the way to supplant the nuclear family. Indeed, for some time the Israelis were certain that the child-care millennium had arrived in their kibbutz day-care centers. Israel seemed to be headed toward the no-family concept.

Today, if we are to believe reports, Israel has clearly decided that the family will be the basic unit of society and not some amorphous institution manned by women substitutes for the mothers who bore these babies.

When and if we move toward extra-utero birth, artificial implantation, and day-care capsules for rearing children, all of what I have written will be cheerfully retracted. I only hope I am not here to see it or say it. That sort of scientific "advance" I respectfully request I be spared.

Mothercraft

There was a time when it was not only fashionable but also well understood that more than one generation of people occupied the same house. Those were the days before World War II, when America hadn't yet discovered suburbia, urban blight, IBM cards, and TV. When young people got married, they often moved into one of their parents' homes. When the newly married couple began to have children, their parents shared in the responsibility of child rearing. Thus, when children became ill, the young wife went to either her mother or her husband's mother and asked what to do. She was told, she did it, and that was the art of practicing mothercraft.

T'aint like that anymore. With the exception of minority groups in America who still practice multi-generational family living, young couples dream of the day when they can separate totally from their families—at least as far as their marital living arrangements are concerned. Thus, when children become ill there isn't anyone to consult except the dear lady living in the next sub-division home—who is also young and inexperienced.

If America needs anything, it is the return to multi-generational living. First of all, there is a severe housing shortage in the country. When and if you can find a house, interest rates are out of sight and sure to go higher. When and if you find a house, there is some strange compulsion to buy more than you can really afford, especially at the beginning of a marriage. And thus, the family is threatened with the worst of all terrors—economic family squabbling.

When the old and the young live together, it is easy to ask Mom what she did when you were sick. Today, since Mom isn't around as much as she used to be, the poor pediatrician gets frantic calls about things that ordinary mothercraft could easily solve.

Here are some interesting facts:

Seventy-five percent of the problems seen by the average pediatrician involve upper respiratory infections. Except for complications and exceptionally high fever, there isn't much more the doctor can do than can the mother. Mothercraft means that parents accept occasional illness as part of the experience of rearing children and that they keep their child in the house, nourished on liquids and aspirin if there is temperature. There is no instant cure. However, in today's world of instant success, instant cooking, instant ecology, and instant credit, many mothers want instant recovery from illness. Indeed, because so many women are in the work force along with their spouses, a sick child at home may mean loss of wages, and perhaps even employment. Doctors are asked for instant cures where there are none. Time and reasonable rest often are the only cures for upper respiratory disease.

Were there a grandmother in the home, the problem

would be solved. One of the great advantages of the multi-generational family is that, where both parents work, there is a very interested party ready and eager to take over in case of a child's illness.

Some folks drop their sick children off, as usual, at nursery school, in spite of the illness and discomfort. When house payments are due and it takes two to make them, the right of the child to the time to get well is often denied. A nursery school of any sort is not the place for a child to be when he has a respiratory infection.

Despite the fact that some mothers-in-law may be difficult to deal with, there is a good case for young couples to consider inviting their parents to live with them as their children grow. The stability of values and the intensity of care the older persons can lavish upon children may be well worth the small inconvenience.

There is no shame in being decent to the people who birthed us. The only shame is the often callous disregard for the loneliness of those who have been relegated to family limbo by America's inordinate desire to live in a "now" generation where only youth is valued.

Mothercraft needs to be taught. It cannot be taught by those who don't know anything about it. It is best taught by someone who cares enough to teach it with love—and your own parents are your best teachers.

There is no need to feel awkward about saying that your folks live with you. I consider it a splendid mark of homage and respect when I know that a couple live happily with the parents of one or even both of the spouses. Honoring one's mother and father means more than an occasional invitation or long-distance call on certain special days.

Becoming human

It has been said—and quite properly, to my way of thinking—that man becomes dehumanized out of the family context. It is only within the limits of a family that the ideal socialization process takes place. Homo sapiens do not develop concern for their fellowmen when they are brought up in institutions or in some strange style, such as the case of the child reared in complete isolation, locked up in a room day and night with no communication with anyone.

The film *John,* a documentary produced in England, focuses on a seventeen-month-old child brought to a residential center for children. Here we see a poignant example of what a difference there is between children from "normal" homes and those reared in institutions. John's mother knew she would have to be in the hospital for quite a few days after the birth of her second child. Having just moved to England and thus being virtually friendless, she found it necessary to put John in a residential center for about nine days.

Despite the fact that John's father visited daily, by the end of seven days this infant was the most devastated child imaginable. For the first day or so he did quite well. The nurses at this facility were excellent, with a ratio of children to nurses about five to one. The food, the sleeping arrangements, and the facilities were good. In short, were a child required to spend time there, no better place could have been provided; short of superb one-family foster care or his own home, this public twenty-four-hour nursery was as well-equipped as any to give custodial care to children.

What was the nature of this care? Essentially, it was the nurses dividing their time as equally as they possibly could among the children in attendance. Children were fed and clothed quite well. The nurses were even reasonably affectionate. But they were not the mothers of these children, nor were they particularly concerned with the total welfare of each child. For the most part, they discharged their duties well, but with a certain detachment.

In one scene of the film *John*, the children are being fed by their nurses. All of the children except John have been at the institution since birth. They have been brought up grabbing for what they can—and grab they do. The place is a bedlam of grabbing, snatching, competitive, argumentative children. John is completely bewildered by all of this, since he had been brought up in a typical modern nuclear family. In his home there were only Mom, Dad, and himself. No one was there to contest for a plate or a cracker. The contrast between the civility of the average home and the frantic bedlam of the group home situation is beautifully shown in this film, which emphasizes the theory that outside the home there is little opportunity to become human.

Out of the family context it is nearly impossible to learn how to be compassionate. The world of the institution, no matter how good that institution is, is really the world of the jungle. Anyone who has been in jail can testify to this. The family tenderizes humans. The family is a necessity so humans don't abandon humanness.

Dr. Margaret Mead said, "As the family goes so goes the nation." America must invest its primary energy in developing better family life rather than better institutions to replace the family.

THE PROBLEMS

The late Professor Howard Lane of San Francisco State University, who was chief psychologist for the Detroit Police Department and the chairman of my doctoral dissertation committee at New York University, used to say in his own Kansas drawl, "Good families and good communities produce good children." The book *The Family Roots of School Learning and Behavior Disorders,* edited by Robert Friedman (Springfield: Charles C. Thomas, 1973), tends to support this proposition. It would be incorrect to say that all problems of children have their origin in the family. It would, on the other hand, be quite correct to say that many of the problems that children manifest have their origins in their family life.

Specifically, Sheldon and Eleanor Glueck, who have described the causes of delinquent behavior, have observed a number of factors that are highly related to the production of delinquent behavior in children. Among these are the protection of the mother, the discipline of the home, the behavior of the father, and others that seem to indicate that one can study the family life of the child and very accurately predict whether or not that child will become a typical delinquent youngster. Literally hundreds of research studies, such as those cited in the Friedman volume, indicate that a great deal of school learning and behavior disorders of children are related to family malpractice.

In a volume written some years ago entitled *Creative Parent-Teacher Conferences,* I called the parent-teacher conference an opportunity for an exchange of information between parents and teachers. Ideally this is so; but by and large, the parent-teacher conference is a time when the teacher tells the parent about what the child is doing or isn't doing socially, academically, vocationally, and otherwise. I have often heard teachers say that after they met the mother or after they met the mother and father or after they met the father alone, they were better able to understand the behavior problems that the child exhibited in school.

For example, we know that children who come from highly authoritarian homes tend to find in school an opportunity to let loose. We find that children from high-achieving homes usually try to achieve greatly in school. Relative to this, for example, a recent United States Office of Education study indicated that when children's parents are college graduates, almost none of them have learning-to-read problems, such as are associated with the children who have parents who are less educated. Children who wish to achieve do not generally become serious behavior problems in school, although my memory is sprinkled with children from affluent and highly educated homes who were extremely difficult to handle. Nonetheless, the case is still strong for the fact that when family life is goal-oriented—that is, when school is important, learning is important, going to college is important—then it is more likely that the children will be imbued with the intense desire to learn and to become; and thus, there is no reason to cause behavior problems in school.

My own experience in teaching in the slums of New York City (before it was fashionable, of course) made this thesis highly evident to me. Where children came from low-achieving homes, from homes where there was the absence of one parent or the other (and in most cases, it was the father), there was a greater degree and a greater intensity of behavioral difficulties in the classroom.

Leon Brill's book *The De-Addiction Process* (Springfield: Charles C. Thomas, 1972) makes it abundantly clear that of the hundreds of addicts whom he studied, he never found a single case in which a youngster became an addict without there being a severe degree of family pathology. This tended to be evidenced by one or the other parent being an alcholic, but even where this was not the case, the behavior of the family was seriously impaired in its everyday transactions.

Freud, Philip Wiley, and others have laid the burden for children's problems directly at the feet of the mother. For years, mothers have suffered the pangs of guilt associated with children who are in trouble. It has been almost as if a father were a nonentity with regard to his influence upon the child's behavioral patterns at home and at school. In the typical family of the 1970s, it is true that the mother tends to be the major influence in the children's upbringing. With the advent of what is known as the women's liberation movement, this seems to be somewhat less evident. We may now expect that fathers will take a more equal share of the burden of "destroying" the children's lives that was assigned to mothers by Dr. Freud.

The severe difficulties a child has with learning in school and behaving at home and in the neighborhood are related to the kinds of home experiences he has had. The Old Testament was eloquent in the matter when it insisted that people have only to teach their children the way in which they should grow, and they will become as they have been taught. While it has recently been fashionable to contradict this, and while it is even possible to find instances of contradiction, it is nonetheless true that what children bring to school and the community from the home plays a clear and definite part in their learning and behavior patterns. Certainly the chapters in this section make it perfectly obvious that the root of problems with regard to school and family behavior, obesity, and drugs often have their origin in the parent-child relationships at home.

Peace at home

Most of the literature about home and family life gives the impression that if life isn't a bowl of cherries, something is wrong with the family. And if something is wrong at home, then surely the fault is with the parents.

Implicit in writings about family life is the assumption that if only the parents knew just a little bit more (say, as much as the writer!), then all would be better. I know this to be true because many an adult has said to my children, "Oh, you are Dr. Landau's child. What is it like to live with an expert?"

My poor wife also faces the many who wonder what life with the "supreme voice of authority" on child-rearing must be like. And it isn't rare for me to be asked how my kids are turning out.

The point is, I have never made any assumption that family life is tranquil. You shouldn't either. It can be incalculably difficult on parents to feel that there must be something wrong with them since there is trouble at home. Family life is filled with alternating peace and tension. It is sheer bliss when all goes well; it is terror when things start exploding. The harried father and mother explain that until their child was fifteen, all was sweetness and light. Suddenly, as if a demon had possessed him, he appears to be no longer theirs but is some sort of diabolic monster who screams revenge in the best tradition of Henry IV.

Family trouble has a way of creeping up without visible signs. Not that the signs aren't there—but it does, on occasion, take a somewhat practiced eye to determine that the future looks a bit bleak.

Just the other day a father told me that until his son was sixteen, he was close to him. The son rarely, if ever, went out at night. All was peaceful until the morning the son called his father and asked him to come home immediately from work. Only then did the father learn that the youth was "all messed up on drugs."

A single cause-and-effect explanation of child behavior is as inappropriate as the same approach to the problems of society. Rarely does A cause B. What is more likely is that there has been a steady and developing accretion of tensions. Too many people expect, both in child-rearing and in marriage, a bliss that is only rarely achievable. When folks try to exist with one another, differences in every conceivable area of concern arise.

In rearing children, the very fact that parents are not dealing with maturity is enough to insure that there will be problems. Early child care is particularly difficult. The demands of the child are inordinate. To try to imagine what bothers the baby is supremely difficult. Mothers, particularly, are saddled with the expectation that they "ought" to know, and fathers expect their wives to be wise about the baby.

The truth of the matter is that mothers (or anyone else) are not given the power to discern and treat the problems of children, except after years of experience.

The real problem is that babies too often are born to inexperienced parents. A young couple, in addition to learning how to survive with one another—and this takes some years—often are raising children at the same time. The combination of wisdom necessary to make both tasks work is almost staggering, and most of it falls squarely upon the mother. So, in her splendid years of youth she must not only be adequate for her infants, but for her husband as well. If the husband is under forty (and most are when their children are young), he has much to learn about reducing his expectations of his poor young wife. And if both would face this terribly difficult issue of pooling their immaturity to benefit the child, then life would immediately be easier.

Far too many young girls in our society carry with them guilt for their inexperience. Far too many young men expect some movie-like atmosphere to pervade a home where reality has left the lunch dishes undone, the babies in various states of disarray.

Peace at home is a process, not an end. Peace at home does not come with a warranty saying that if not satisfied, the merchandise may be returned for a full adjustment. When there is peace at home—and there can be much—be assured that it is valued and remembered by all. When there isn't, it doesn't mean failure.

Be it ever so hollow

Within a 100-yard radius of my friend's house are five families who have been or are in the process of becoming unglued.

In one a woman deserted three young daughters—not to run off with another man, not to escape the brutality of a husband, but to find herself.

In another, an unfulfilled man who, like Willy Loman in the play *Death of a Salesman*, never quite lived up to a vast potential, finally decided to try the world alone.

In a third, money and good fortune aroused a dormant lust for others.

In a fourth, a militant father who knew what was right for everyone but himself saw each of his children depart from the prescribed path in defiance of cherished values. These values were flagrantly tattooed upon young foreheads, only to fade when the tattooer turned his back.

Finally, there is a bloated drug-ridden father who survives each day in a haze of legal prescriptions.

If this is the truth in a middle-sized midwestern community, if this is the state of the family along the shores of the implacable Mississippi, how, one might ask, can I continue to defend today's family?

Not too long ago a documentary series entitled *The American Family* was seen on television, featuring a family with the surname Loud. Those who saw any or all of the segments in this series may have some comprehension of the conditions in a family that can cause the misery noted above, through seeing the horrendous life the Loud family lived. The Louds were not poor; they were not racially "wrong"; they were not undereducated. They were none of the things we too often associate with failing families.

Since the days of Cain and Abel the family has been in trouble. It will always be difficult to rear fine families. A close look at the Loud family showed what was missing in their mix. I defend the family because it is never too late to switch horses.

A television crew invaded the Loud family in Santa Barbara, California, with their consent. In the seven months they were in residence the cameras recorded the breakup of a twenty-year marriage, the flamboyant homosexuality of the eldest son, a brush fire nearby that threatened to destroy their home, the demise of the husband's business, and the laziness of the youngest son.

By many present-day standards the family was a reasonable success. Its members were educated, affluent, handsome. True, a son had chosen a different life-style, but many avant-garde families might tolerate this.

Nothing in the world touched this family. Aside from regular and continual social drinking, little was said about anything of any significance. They were linked to no one but themselves, and not very tightly there. No real love between daughter and father existed except on the telephone. No one was emotionally sick except the homosexual son, yet no one was very well.

The family united in nothing. There was no concern for the world of migrant workers, for the war dead, for philosophy; there was no religion, no ethic, no moral right or wrong, no sense of judgment.

More importantly, when the series of twelve episodes ended, the viewer had seen enough to wish he could "go and sin no more" himself.

Family conflict and school behavior

Everything that happens in a family affects everyone in that family. This is a very simple but accurate statement.

Once having accepted this truism, it is obvious that some school difficulties that children experience are likely to come from the conditions that exist at home. When there is chronic antagonism between parents and children, bad feelings are stored in the child's psyche, and these frustrations and antagonisms are very likely to spill over into hostile or aggressive behavior in school.

It isn't unusual for a child to feel a certain amount of guilt for bad relationships at home. It is strange how folks, children included, develop feelings of responsibility for things over which they have no influence. In other words, while a child isn't responsible for the incapacity of one of his brothers or sisters, it isn't unusual for him to feel responsible. These bad feelings at home can channel themselves into bad behavior at school.

I have been interested in the phenomena of people who act out in society or school so much that the entire school or neighborhood is aware of their antisocial behavior. I don't mean the child who on occasions runs afoul of school authority. I refer to those whose behavior is nearly always aggressive. What has intrigued me is the incidence of authority conflict at home where there is so frequently a harsh, punitive, and rejecting parent.

When children are engaged in continual struggles for power at home, they often test the authority of their teachers by being aggressive in school.

Many years ago there was a rash of murders of young women by an individual who always left a note in lipstick saying, "Stop me before I kill more." Many people who do antisocial things—especially children—flag society, their parents, or their teachers by doing so much wrong that it is inevitable that they get caught, or they leave enough clues about so that we conclude they are begging to be caught. Parental overpermissiveness produces few inner controls, and the child is unable to brake his overt aggression. Often misbehavior is the signal that no one is saying no, that no one cares enough to put an end to aggressive behavior. Many children are pleading for an effective authority to respond and help.

On the other hand, an overly strict home environment may force a child into hostile behavior at school as an outlet. Many children will let loose in other places when there is repressiveness in the home atmosphere. When a "double-bind message" is sent from parents to child—a message that says one thing on the surface, but another message is implicit—there is bound to be trouble.

For instance, the parents may say that school is important and that the rules must be obeyed—but they don't respond to teachers who ask to see them. They flagrantly violate rules, and thus they send the hidden message that rules are for suckers. As a result, the child has the great disadvantage of being wrong no matter what he does. If he obeys rules, he is good-but-stupid; if he doesn't, he is smart-but-bad. So he opts not to abide by any rules, or he acts as if they weren't there in the first place.

Everything that has been said so far regarding children applies equally to adults. Marital conflict, overauthority of one parent to another, overpermissiveness of one adult with another, and double-binding between husband and wife all serve to affect the quality of work performance of both individuals. A human being cannot produce the best that is within him when his at-home conflicts are paralyzing.

All humans need folks who level with them about most matters. Too tight a rein is as bad as too loose a rein. We all need reasonable restraints; we all need to feel the winds of freedom blowing through ourselves. When the balance is tipped in favor of one or the other, it is like squeezing the end of a toothpaste tube with the cap on. The paste will come out someplace—usually from a seam—and it is thus wasted. And so it is with human resources that are pressured with no outs allowed.

School behavior problems and the family

It is axiomatic among schoolteachers that the children whose parents need most to be at the parent-teacher conference are never there.

Hostile, aggressive children don't get that way by accident. They have to learn their hostilities, and they learn many of them from home. It wouldn't take much probing to discover that the children causing most of the problems in school, especially those related to resisting authority figures, have one or both parents who claim that they, too, never got on with their teachers.

Not too long ago a great fuss was made over the general nonconformity of children in the schools. This was an era when schools took to task boys with long hair. Americans over forty generally distrusted long hairs. Most of these nonconformist children came from homes where their dads and moms decided to ignore their own age—they were going to be part of the younger generation by dressing and acting as modishly as their sons and daughters. When the expressed family value is nonconformity, one cannot expect much from children.

Problems also arise when the overall communication pattern at home is not clear. Then children learn to assume meanings. If their parents do not mean what they say or do not say what they mean, then the child learns to distrust communication. When he basically distrusts what he hears at home, then at school he has no particular reason to take at face value what teachers say.

Where there is stress in a family, school behavior is especially affected. Often this is merely temporary stress—a new baby on the scene, a difficult relocation, a temporary illness, or a short-lived loss of income. When the stress is removed, almost everything goes back to normal.

A large percentage of children who are behavior problems come from families where there is divorce, separation, death of a parent, remarriage, desertion, etc. Divorce is probably the most difficult experience the child lives with. There is no simple way to explain what is happening. Some marital situations are very difficult, and keeping the marriage together is not the best thing for the children. Yet, no matter how bad things are, the children do suffer as parents fight for custody, make awkward visiting arrangements, and try to build new lives upon the ashes of the past.

The terrible effect an alcoholic parent has upon a family is well known. The "family secret" is never a secret very long, and the child often has to face the slings and arrows of outrageous peers who quite deliberately twist the knife in the wound.

A crisis in the family that is not often described or defined and is not fully understood is the case of "school phobia" or "school refusal." Most often the child is seen as the culprit here. It is the child, they say, who won't leave the mother to remain in school. However, it is not really the child who can't leave the mother, but the mother who can't leave the child—though her overt messages are that the child should not be afraid to stay in school.

In these cases, most often teachers and harried principals work desperately with the child, who is seen as the one to blame. Actually, it's the mother who needs help, so that she does not continue to emit double messages. On the one hand she says, "Go, my child; stay in school." And on the other hand she really can't let go, and this is the message that is conveyed to the child.

The family matrix is not a simple one. It pervades the very being of children. It is often at the root of school failure. Let's free the children from bearing the full weight of guilt about misbehavior at school. It takes two to tango. It takes more than a child to create a behavior problem in school.

Fat kids

Know what? Writing about families and children could be fun except that every once in a while you really put your thumb in your ear. You see, it's easy to talk in generalities—you can't go too far wrong. But, not everyone who reads what you write knows that you may not be talking about their children or their families, so the next thing you know you have hurt someone you really love just because you have made some fairly solid generalizations.

Shall I prove my point? Okay, I have never seen a really fat child who has "glandular problems." I have never seen a fat child who did not have one or more obese parents. I have never seen a fat child who has not been encouraged to eat by one or both parents.

But you have, you say? So be it. I'm wrong. Now, I haven't seen all of the fat children in the world, but the ones I have seen are too often eating many things they shouldn't.

Let's get away for a moment from the realm of personal experience. After all, one observer doesn't make a case. Here are some things that are quite well documented.

First, fat children are as unhappy about their weight as are adults, at least in the American culture. We are a nation that stresses sleekness. Sleek children are as adored as are sleek adults. Fat children are made fun of. Their peers are unmerciful, their teachers often unwittingly say things to them that hurt, and their parents are angry with them because they aren't svelte. To top it off, they are unhappy with themselves because they are so different.

It is the cruelest of beliefs to imagine that there is any truth to the idea that fat people are naturally happy. Where the society does not value fatness, it takes a very idiosyncratic person indeed to be happy and bubbly. If there is any large measure of happiness, it is likely to be a cover-up to a great deal of sadness. This is not to say that there are no fat children who aren't happy. It is to state that given the conditions of our culture today, such normal happiness is unlikely.

It is as difficult to motivate the fat child to want to lose weight as it is for the average adult to start the slimming process. With obese children, there is a more complicated problem than that faced by the ordinary obese adult. That problem is that one or both of his parents, despite their wish to have him lose weight, also send him double messages.

On the one hand, they probably have equated eating with health. You may recall how skittish you were with your first child. If you didn't breast-feed, you probably spent many anxious moments feeding, holding the bottle up to the light to see how many ounces the baby took. Few of us have implicit faith in the fact that babies stop eating when they are full. But with bottle-fed babies, there is the constant concern for finishing a certain number of ounces despite the fact that few children ever starve to death when there is constant food available.

At any rate, we consider that a gaining, even heavy, baby is better than a light one. Notice how we announce birth weight with each birth announcement card we write. We take a certain pride in higher birth weights rather than lower ones.

Few children are motivated to lose weight, so parental observation and control are important. The difficulty here is that parents mean well, even say that the child is too heavy, but deep within them there is conflict. Weight equals health. How can one deprive the child of food?

By the sixth and seventh years some children may exhibit really conscious obesity. Certainly by the age of eleven or so the problem is very serious, since puberty is just around the corner. Here we have the most advantageous conditions for slimming down. When slimming is a result of parent castigation and pressure, there is only a perfunctory compliance with diets. It is really only when the obese child himself wants to lose weight that there is the best chance for success. It isn't at all unlike the young girl who never lifted a pot cover until the day before she was married; the intensity with which she will now attend to her mother's cooking instruction is unbelievable!

It is urgent that parents, once they have resolved to no longer send double messages, remember not to compare fat children with other siblings or peers. When a parent's love and affection is contingent upon the "proper" size, it's sort of like going into the boxing ring with someone who outweighs you. No child can combat (emotionally, that is) a problem if he knows that his beating the problem is a matter of gaining or losing the love of his parents. We need to love the child despite his size, yet be healthy enough ourselves to be catalysts in a therapeutic way to the process of weight loss.

The obese child needs to adopt certain patterns of speech in order to combat the temptation to eat the various goodies offered him in life. It is wise to claim that you are allergic to all fattening foods. When offered a Napoleon, it is prudent to say that you are allergic to it. It is true. If you eat it, you will break out in fat.

Obesity in children

In our slim-minded society, fatness is a curse, It wasn't always that way.

In Shakespeare's *Julius Caesar*, we hear, "Yond' Cassius has a lean and hungry look;/He thinks too much; such men are dangerous." Earlier Caesar said, "Let me have men about me that are fat."

There are still tribes in Africa where women are, for some weeks prior to marriage, kept in little huts and fed lavishly so they will gain weight and thus be more attractive. Only in the Occidental world is there such a preoccupation with fatness that there are major industries devoted exclusively to helping folks lose weight.

Fat children suffer from the scorn and ridicule heaped upon them by their peers and often by the adults in their family—but not all of the adults. It seems that some thirty years ago Hilda Bruch, a physician at Columbia University's College of Physicians and Surgeons, did her first studies on obese children and discovered some things that seem to be directly related to the child's family and particularly to the mother. In 1970, and still today, her work is cited, often with some rebuttal from her colleagues. She said, "Close, personal contact with fat children reveals...that they are not just overweight and jolly, as has been popularly assumed, but that they suffer from serious disturbances in their behavior and personality.....

"Both the abnormal food habits and disturbed personality development are related to disturbing experiences within a family." *(The Child in His Family,* New York: John Wiley & Sons, 1970.)

However, it would be a miscarriage of justice to assume, without evidence, that all fat children are the result of a disturbed parent-child relationship. It appears more likely to be true to say that frequently obese children are that way because they have been overfed by mothers who are unduly concerned for their health and welfare. It would also be perfectly fair to say that few fat children are fat because of endocrine (glandular) disorders.

Thirty years ago Dr. Bruch discovered that it was not endocrine misfunction that was the cause of obesity. She concluded that the "hovering, anxious behavior of the mothers and their resistance against changing any aspect of a child's life, in particular the excessive eating, suggested the possibility of some disturbance in the psychological climate of these families."

It was particularly interesting then, and it still is of special interest to me, that the father's role in obesity was conspicuous by its absence. Mothers who had severely overweight children were bundles of unfulfilled aspirations and had suffered in their own childhoods from poverty, hunger, and insecurity, according to Dr. Bruch's report. Most felt that they had been left to fend for themselves too early, and the maternal responses to these conditions were self-pity, resentment, and overinvolvement with their children.

In the absence of contrary information, the Bruch syndrome appears to me to be reasonable but not necessarily the case in all instances. In other words, when adults get down on themselves, they often overeat. Tension and anxiety create the need to release energy, and where such outlets are impossible, it isn't at all unusual to gorge with more food than we ordinarily need.

When the same tension, poor self-image, etc., are present in a mother, especially one who has a young child, it seems entirely possible that gratification may come from an offspring who is made happy through overattention and love. This often is equivalent to feeding the child more than he needs, under the presumption that if some is good, more is better.

In reporting her findings, Dr. Bruch said: "It was felt that the fundamental rejection which many mothers felt toward their children was overcompensated by overprotective measures and excessive feeding, and that, in a home environment without emotional security, food had been endowed with an exaggerated importance and was charged with a high emotional value, substituting for love, security, and satisfaction." ("The Family Frame of Obese Children," *Psychosomatic Medicine,* April 1940.)

Dr. Bruch determined that frequently the mother had hoped for a girl to become a companion to her and instead had a boy, whom she rejected and thus fed to make up for her disappointment.

You don't get fat unless you eat more than you use. In the feeding of an infant, where most obesity really starts, the cooperation of another person (usually the mother) is demanded. This means that the child cannot overeat unless he is overfed, and this overindulgent feeding is the beginning of obesity.

Fat kids, then, are helped by some adult to become fat. Though not always true, it is more than likely accurate.

Who are the "street people"?

After the flower children left San Francisco, they were followed by the "street people."

The flower children had gathered in San Francisco to celebrate the possibility of sharing the good life together. These folks sought to live for an ideal that fizzled, as all Utopian schemes are wont to do. The street people, on the other hand, are the nomads of America. They are very unhappy adolescents, some 18 to 20, others 40 and over, still adolescents in that they longingly search for an identity that they have never quite come to terms with during their post-adolescent years.

There are a number of similarities between flower children and street people. The essential difference is that street people have left home to escape a very painful situation, rather than to regain a lost innocence.

When the Educational Alliance studied 500 street people, they came up with some bizarre and awesome findings. Here are some of them: Seventy-five percent of the group studied belonged to middle-class and lower middle-class families. Over 75 percent of the total population came from the northeast section of the U.S. Fifty-five percent came from suburban communities; 40 percent came from large metropolitan areas other than New York. Only five percent came from small towns.

The average age range was from 14-24. The population was 90 percent white, four percent black. Fifty-five percent were Protestant, 30 percent Jewish, and 15 percent Catholic.

Nearly 60 percent of the group came from homes where one of the original parents was not present. Twelve percent came from orphanages or other institutions and foster homes. The average age for leaving home was 16.

One of the more interesting figures is that "60 percent of the group reported the absence of one of their original parents." This, of course, does not mean that divorce, death, or separation dooms a child to becoming a street person. It does suggest rather strongly that when there is severe trauma prior to the age of 16, its effects upon the personality development of children can be cataclysmic.

Growing up and into maturity is difficult enough as it is, especially when you have been raised in populous places where anonymity is prevalent. Note that few rural kids run to the streets, perhaps because they feel the kinship of the small town. The feeling of nothingness ever present in large cities, coupled with the loss of a parent for whatever reason, is sufficient to combine forces and do harm to the integration of a child's personality.

The report tells us that virtually every youngster who was lacking one of his original parents gave that deficit as an underlying factor in his leaving home. But the story doesn't end quite that simply. The street people go on to report that upon the remarriage of the remaining parent, there was the tendency for the new partner to take over and adopt the role of enforcer and punisher. This exaggerated the feelings of rejection the child had for the intruder in his life and added to his feelings of alienation from both parents. Under these circumstances, it isn't too difficult to understand the deep feelings of resentment that led to his eventually adopting the role of nomad.

It is very important for adolescents to develop their identity in a known, loving, and accepting environment. When children leave home and continue the process of individualization in a community characterized by an extreme absence of norms and a high degree of transiency and mobility, they are deprived of the opportunity to develop in a healthy way.

Even though there is much tumultuousness in many homes where adolescents are developing, this should be considered normal, and it is urgent for parents to understand that as difficult as it may be, it is better for the child to grow up with some combat at home than to grow up in the streets of some city where the only folks who seem to care are others of the same age.

I wish parents could take this last line and read it together with their children who may be about to split. As bad as home may seem to be, there is not one shred of reliable evidence that communal or street life gives any lasting satisfaction.

One of my good friends, an unusually gifted psychiatrist, often says that it is our lies that eventually destroy us. Before contemplating the "idyllic" life on the street, youngsters ought to sit down with their parents and agree to examine the fibs they both believe about themselves and each other. The process of starting from way back and tracing the sources of dissension between parents and children is a painful and difficult one. The lies by which we may have lived need to be exposed. If this is done with honesty on both sides of the fence, the process alone can be healing.

Let's look at some of the grim figures about what really awaits a teenager out on the street. Three out of five street people studied had severe psychiatric problems, and half of them had been hospitalized. Two-thirds of them had a history of psychosomatic disease. Two-thirds had a history of infectious disease and had been hospitalized.

Forty percent of the group who were older than 20 had gonorrhea and 14 percent had a history of hepatitis. Well over half of the population had a history of over three different disease categories. Nearly half of the girls had been pregnant. And, of course, the use of drugs was widespread.

The street people are unhappy children who have rejected home and sought refuge in large city streets. The evidence is clear that all they find is infinite corridors of despair. They are seeking fulfillment of unmet needs. Sixty percent of them have suffered family disruption.

Families need to allow growth and fulfillment within the family structure, and there is no simple formula. Listening and love, understanding and even compassion are essential.

Youth values need to be understood by parents even if they are not shared. As difficult as this is to accomplish, there is only one place where it should happen. The family is still the only viable answer to the problem of growing up sane.

The streets and communes offer little but grim rewards.
 Stay home, my children, and fight it out if necessary. There is nothing much better outside your family, even if it's pretty tough.

Drug disease— what's the cure?

In 1804 morphine was lauded as the cure for opium addiction. In 1904 heroin was lauded as the cure for morphine addiction. In 1964 methadone was lauded as the cure for heroin addiction. We have not learned from our mistakes.

In New York City alone 60,000 addicts are enrolled in methadone programs, and 30,000 addicts are on waiting lists. A projected goal of 150,000 additional addicts to be enrolled is part of the great plan.

Now is not the time to find someone to blame for our addicted society. What shall we do with the countless thousands of children and adults who are afflicted with this dread disease? Addiction is a disease pure and simple. It is not the product of a warped and evil mind. It is foisted and fostered by every segment of our society.

Two pediatricians in Brooklyn, New York, interviewed 300 women at their clinic. They went through their handbags and in half of them they found headache remedies, nerve pills, tranquilizers, vitamins, nitroglycerine, diet pills, saccharin, and contraceptive pills. This shouldn't shock you; it should awaken you to the simple fact that interest in drugs is not relegated to only that segment of society that wears long hair and split jeans with frayed ends. If you don't believe me, go into your own purse right now and see what's there. Better still, amble over to your medicine cabinet and count the number of bottles of pills that are there.

If you are still not convinced that drugs are a way of life in America for those in every class and caste, just check with your neighbor about the various well-educated, distinguished members of your community who recently joined the acid-heads under twenty-one.

Addiction is curable. It is merely a difficult disease like many other forms of illness, both psychiatric and medical, such as cancer and heart disease.

An article in *Time* magazine December 11, 1972, entitled "A Glimmer of Light," created the impression that drug addiction is not curable. The article starts out discussing the epidemic of drug abuse in America and then goes on to laud a program to counteract drug abuse—methadone maintenance—as a boon to mankind.

In 1964, when methadone was first recommended, one might have made a nodding agreement, since methadone is specific to heroin. In 1973, heroin is nearly passing from the scene, and modern drug users are not content with one drug—they use four and five simultaneously. In fact, according to recent Food and Drug Administration guidelines, those using many drugs at one time are ineligible for methadone maintenance.

What is the answer to our drug disease?

For whatever reason, drug addicts usually are people who hold themselves in very low esteem. They are sick children who have turned away from the real world and retreated into a never-never land where they do not have to face themselves. They have chosen the easy way out of solving life's problems. Whether they are members of the professional community (and thousands are) or of the Third World culture, whether they are tired and disappointed homemakers or juvenile dropouts from life, they all share the same symptoms.

The only answer that makes any sense is to dot the American landscape with psychiatrically oriented, drug-free therapeutic communities where the diseased person spends at least eighteen months learning to face his life, his peers, and the world realistically. Substituting one addiction for another, such as methadone for heroin, is not one whit different from trying to cure an alcoholic by substituting scotch for wine or gin.

Dr. Edward Senay, director of the Illinois Drug Abuse Programs, has said that an addict has a 95 percent probability of returning to drugs if he has been abstinent for a period of time. Abstinence without the therapy of a long-term confrontation with oneself is a guarantee of a return. Substituting one drug for another never gets at the root of the problem.

It would be unfair of me not to inform you of my particular bias in this respect. More than a year ago I was offered $10,000 by a grandmother if I could find a cure for her grandson's addiction. I set about investigating every type of program and concluded that the therapeutic, drug-free community known as Odyssey House was the best answer. Hard work, personal confrontation, a no-nonsense approach to infractions of rules, no pity for one's past, and an eighteen-month stay in residence added up to a realistic attack upon a terrible disease. I finally joined the national board of directors of Odyssey. (Incidentally, the young man then and now refuses any part of treatment.)

If I had my way, I would forcibly, if necessary, round up addicts and give them at least a month's taste of Odyssey House. Some critics wish only to put addicts away for life. Diseased people don't need jails. They need help in getting their heads on straight. Crash pads and bleeding hearts only compound the disease. Cries of "Hang them" are as hideous as those who sob for the civil rights of these sick people, who are endangering not only their own lives but also the welfare of the still unborn.

The right not to participate in therapeutic programs is a dubious one. One's rights end where the health and welfare of others start. Simplistic solutions to life's complexities appear to be waiting for instant implementation. A therapeutic community beats the asphalt jungle any time.

The families of drug addicts

In Dr. Leon Brill's study entitled *The De-Addiction Process* (Springfield: Charles C. Thomas, 1972), he describes the characteristics of the typical family of the addict. Focus must be made upon the mother and father of the addict. Their marriage and their personalities are inextricably bound up in the causes of addiction.

Lest anyone draw the erroneous conclusion that the condition I shall describe *must* lead to producing addicted children, let me enter an immediate disclaimer. Unlike the work of Sheldon and Eleanor Glueck, who have been able to predict juvenile delinquency with some 85 percent accuracy, no such reliability in predicting future addicts is available. Nonetheless, it is true that the likelihood of producing addicted children increases if the following family factors are present.

First, when there is evidence of "emotional divorce" between the parents, with each of them choosing a favorite child, we have one of the indispensable ingredients of the necessary family mix that is likely to lead to drug-addicted children. "Emotional divorce" refers to couples who occupy the same premises and share bed and board as married folks are expected to do, but who are, in spirit, divorced. They live together for any number of reasons, but they are not positively emotionally involved.

Next, an overprotective, seductive mother adds to the factors necessary toward contributing to the creation of the addicted child. The overprotection factor means that the child's early life experiences were too carefully monitored not by a mean person, but rather by a mother who was overly emotionally involved with her child (usually a son). The seductiveness of the mother may or may not be related to the overprotectiveness. That is, an overprotective mother is not necessarily seductive. A seductive mother, on the other hand, is nearly always overprotective. The relationship between the overprotectiveness and seductiveness and the emotional divorce is, I trust, fairly obvious.

Dr. Brill describes the typical father of the addict: "What is fairly typical, or at least frequent, is the existence of an alcoholic father who serves as a prototype for drug abuse or impulsive living." *(The De-Addiction Process*, p. 71.) Also not too unusual is a symbiotic relationship between, most often, the mother and child. At the same time, the father is either emotionally absent or is incompetent due to his own alcoholic addiction.

No appropriate role model is afforded the child, who then turns to his peer group for guidance. When there is no end of a parent's doing for his or her child, when there is an exorbitant gratification derived from meeting the needs of the child (symbiosis), the lengths to which that parent will go are unbelievable. Brill reports about a mother who actually arranged to furnish drugs to her son for his own use or to sell. At first reading, this may be utterly incomprehensible to the average parent. Yet, the denial parents engage in is legendary. I have seen documented evidence, time and again, of parents having children who "shoot up" at home and who bring home the things they have just stolen to support their habit, with nary a word from either parent.

Surprising?

Consider the millions of so-called good parents who drink with their children and leave liquor and pills within easy reach. I have heard reports of "with it" parents who smoke grass with their kids with the mistaken idea that they are sharing life with them. If it takes an energy crisis to force folks to be at home with their children, so be it. Even such a crisis is not likely to teach a parent how to love and communicate below the level of superficiality.

I have never known an addicted person who was able to honestly say that his family was a great institution. I have never heard any drug addict report that his relationships with his folks were super but that he rejected the ideal atmosphere.

Kids can grow well in poverty, amid social turmoil, even war, if the place they call home is more than a house. None of us can be perfect parents; we all goof plenty. But if we love each other, and the kids see it or sense it or know it in some way, they are less likely to drop out of that world into the hell that is the dope fiend's every-day "heaven."

The real danger of marijuana

I suspect it will take a few more years of concentrated research to get final and definitive answers regarding the real harm that marijuana can do to the human body. There is, however, enough evidence available to convince me that its harmful effects are clear and present. Enough marijuana and hashish entered the United States in 1973 to make about five billion individual joints or cigarettes. Assuming for a moment that it is only fanatic fundamentalist jabberwocky that indicts marijuana, is there anything else about its use that is worrisome? There are two very important things that must be candidly said:

1. The chemical composition of marijuana in and of itself does not lead to the use of other drugs, but the use of marijuana by early and mid-adolescents is likely to lead to experimenting with other drugs.

Physical effects aside for a moment, the protracted and steady use of marijuana or hashish eventually leads the human being into a state of dependence (not to be termed addiction).

My firsthand acquaintance with drug addicts in seven

states leads me to say that in 98 percent of the cases of addiction to hard stuff, marijuana was tried first. Now, don't jump to any hasty conclusions here. This is not a cause-and-effect situation. That is, marijuana is not the cause of heroin addiction. In the age group 11-23, the adolescent subculture, as it were, it is very likely that first-time experimenters will escape the effects of the drug. If he has tried marijuana one time and left it alone from then on, the adolescent or early pubescent will be home free except for the fact that he "smoked behind the barn." But it isn't that simple. Few experimenters can let it go at that.

In the teenage culture, where the market is very large, there is always bound to be someone around who exhorts the teenybopper to "try something with a real bang." The dare, the challenge is nearly irresistible to the youngster. The real bang may be heroin, amphetamines, LSD, methadone, or any one of a dozen other drugs. Thus, where there is marijuana around, it is more likely that other drugs will be around.

This is what I would tell any youngster who is suspected of dabbling. Scare tactics, threats, and similar approaches don't work. A frank look at where the scene is will work lots better. And if none of this has any effect, send him to an Odyssey House and they'll set him straight.

My experience is with multiple drug users. None—or very few—started with heroin. The road to hard drugs is strewn with marijuana joints, mother's diet pills, dad's pep pills, and whiskey from someone's liquor cabinet.

Much of the adolescent's completely baffling behavior is related to his desperate search for himself in these crucial years, his search for identity. He is trying his personality and coping techniques out on the family and the peer world in which he lives.

If he emerges with clear answers to the questions of who he is, where he is going, and what awaits him once there, then he has successfully passed through adolescence. In other words, this time between eleven and twenty-three is a problem-solving time. There are hurts, joys, failures, some successes. If, perchance, marijuana becomes a way of life in these years, there is also a psychological dependence upon the drug.

What this really means is that the teenager will not try to cope with life. He will drop out of the conflict and resolve his problems by drifting off into a drugged stupor, which temporarily makes him forget what is bugging him—a pleasant but deadly way to circumvent normal development.

The alcoholic also has decided to turn away from the hassles of life and find his comfort in being drugged. This is not an evil person; it is one person's answer to life's persistent inquiry into our psyche. It is no way to live life.

Drug addicts are not evil humans. They are children eating too much honey. They are very sick and need help as much as do those with ulcers and obesity.

Dead from overdose

The corpse of the nineteen-year-old boy lay stiff on the hideaway bed. The rest of the East 85th Street apartment was filled with assorted females who were, in one way or another, a part of the dead boy's past. There were no men present except a policeman from the 19th precinct; Dr. Michael Baden, the deputy medical examiner of New York City; and I.

Earlier in the evening my host, Dr. Baden, had been asked to swing around to an apartment nearby where the body of an apparently O.D.'d (overdosed) young man had been lying on its death bed since 2:30 in the afternoon. And so, since I was in New York for a quarterly meeting of the Odyssey House board of directors, Dr. Baden invited me to watch the coroner's work in this situation from start to finish. As we bundled into an official car and sped the few blocks to our destination, Dr. Baden told me that in any case of unnatural death, there must be a coroner on the scene, and now we were on the scene.

An immediate and cursory examination showed a cone-like froth excretion around the boy's mouth—some indication of an opiate. His body showed no evidence of tracks on the arms; he wasn't mainlining heroin. But we did gather up four bottles of assorted pills, and since the history and examination taken by the coroner showed no recent heroin use, a tentative conclusion, based upon testimony given us by the boy's mother concerning his drug habits, was that the youngster died because of an overdose of methadone and other drugs. (Methadone is given medically as an alternative to heroin. In Utah it is dispensed to nearly 300 heroin addicts on a day-to-day basis. It is as addictive as heroin.)

What of the lad's past history? The mother, long divorced, said he began his drug addiction by sniffing glue. He then graduated to marijuana, experimented with hallucinogens, and at sixteen became hopelessly addicted to heroin.

After nearly two years in an anti-drug program, he split and headed for Florida and the free and easy life of a drug addict. He never held a job very long. He dug counterculture music, art, and literature, and for the past six months he had been living with his mother's best friend, a woman twenty years his senior.

I listened to everything—hours of endless detail of a life wasted by drugs. Drug addiction, now not so specific as in days past, is more likely to be addiction to a wide spectrum of substances. One takes drugs such as heroin and alcohol to forget, to turn away from whatever reality exists in one's private world. It is the adolescent way of withdrawing from the real world and retreating into one's self in some desperate search or meaning, and the only meaning found is in drugs. The addict finds no happiness or peace in others, in himself, or in anything but his needle and his ceaseless search for a supply of drugs.

The search, for any of those who may be tinkering with the notion of splitting the straight life for the drug subculture, is one of the most enervating, disheartening street adventures possible. There is no end. All day, all night the addict scrounges the streets, if not to steal, then to buy his supply. And throughout all of this frantic searching for money (the habit costs as much as $150 per day), the addict has to keep one eye open for the narcs (police on the narcotics squad). What a life for a nineteen-year-old!

As far as I could gather there had never been a significant male figure in this boy's life. Now, I have no evidence that male teachers teach boys more or better, but I am quite certain that interested, warm, and humane men can become very significant in the lives of pre-addicted youth.

As I thought of these things, the men from the city morgue rolled the leaden, inflexible body of what was once a little boy into the canvas bag that would envelop him until the stone slab at the morgue could replace it. The little fat man who made the final folds in the canvas gingerly, if not daintily, removed the beaded necklaces from the corpse's neck and wrist. Then he turned to the bewildered mother, shrugged, and picked up his end of the stretcher. The new bracelet-tag read O.D., followed by the boy's name. The lady from next door touched my arm and said, "Yunno, he wuz a sweet kid."

Happiness without drugs

Man's quest has always been for personal happiness. Despite sporadic temporary searches, such as space exploration or gold seeking, it may be fairly said that his search is for happiness. When parents are asked what they most want for their children, there is an amazing uniformity of response. Few ask for riches. Most want success; all want happiness.

For some, happiness is a warm puppy. For others, happiness is riches. For the drug addict, happiness is a fix.

When folks continue taking drugs, it is usually because of a diseased ego, one that does not have the strength to believe in itself as an entity. Most addicts stay with their addictions so they can remain in a happy state, obliterating the world and its woes.

There will always be tragedy, disappointment, and suffering in life. Happiness is not a warm puppy or marriage to a beauty queen. It is a state of existence that derives from acknowledging that beautiful moments are to be cherished because they are rare.

Our aspirin age has too frequently retreated to the taking of some pill that will take away the headache and the heartache, sometimes both at once. It is only when people face tragedy with the idea that the challenge they are facing is greater than their human resources that it becomes necessary for them to hit the bottle or the hypodermic.

If the challenge of asking for a raise is too great, bourbon will do, at least until the awful moment is over. If the challenge of a difficult marriage is too great, then resorting to the company of others may provide instant relief. Three martinis before dinner may make most home problems fade nearly into obscurity.

Self-doubt makes achieving happiness impossible, so it is natural to resort to whatever temporary measures will assuage the gnawing feelings of unhappiness. In other words, what will turn an addict around is the knowledge that feeling good now isn't as important as feeling good for a long time.

The only satisfying way of life for the addict is one continual fix after another, where momentary happiness comes and goes. And when the addict learns through therapy and his peers that drug-induced feelings of happiness are short-lived, he starts to focus on learning new skills that will displace the need for immediate happiness.

The easy way out in the treatment of addiction is drug therapy. The most difficult way is no drugs—and most folks won't, don't, and can't wait for cures under this regime. Anything less is not criminal or wilful neglect. It is superficial and expedient. No one can be truly happy in a drugged state even if that state is vastly superior to what it was before.

The greatest happiness comes when one is drug-free and

self-actualizing. When a person thinks enough of himself to cope with himself, he is happy. This does not mean that man must make his own happiness unaided by others. Help is important, especially help from concerned people.

THE STRENGTHS

One of the fundamental premises of this book is that if family problems are part of the causation for the behavior problems of children and youth, then it is possible to learn how to build a strong family so that the chances of your child's becoming delinquent or developing a severe emotional problem will be minimized. A further premise is that family problems may be studied and that parents can take actions that will ameliorate the broken family communication patterns that usually result in school and home behavior problems.

Unlike the many nostrums in this field that claim to teach a jargon or special language that will guarantee successful families and children, this volume does not operate on the premise that there is a secret formula, a special jargon that will do the trick. It proceeds from the viewpoint that there are some rather fundamental ways to deal with children within the family structure that make sense. They do not require the learning of a new language, nor do they require a bold and vast change of life-style. They *do* envision a reflective view of the family by each member of that family, consultation, especially between parents about their view(s) of their family and their children, and the understanding of some of the fundamentals of communication that are essential to therapeutic child rearing.

Actually, in this book the home is viewed as somewhat of a therapeutic community. It is a place where it is safe to grow, where the parents understand the significance of listening, and where the children understand that they have responsibilities and obligations just as their parents do.

There are those who will find within these pages what they may wish to term a behavior modification approach. Well, if behavior modification is paying a great deal of attention and giving a great deal of approval for the things that children do that parents wish to see repeated, then so be it. There are those who will see shades of Rogerian analysis, of Gordon's methodology, or of Haim Ginott. To the extent that this is seen by readers, so be it. I have been essentially a disciple of Howard Lane, whom many have termed a human dynamicist. He was a psychologist who did his graduate work at the University of Chicago and was essentially a humanist in the field of child growth and behavior. Any disciple worth his salt will take his master's words, exemplify them, build upon them, and then develop his own philosophy.

My psychology is not any one person's; it's certainly not my own in the sense of its belonging to me and originating with me. As far as I can tell, the Family Interaction Grid, as it is described in this section, is uniquely my own and a technique that I have taught to a few hundred graduate students in psychology, social work, medicine, and law. It does not claim uniqueness for its theoretical construct, but it does claim uniqueness for its specificity and methodology. For those who are "do-it-yourselfers," it offers great possibilities. For those who don't believe they can go it alone and who think that they need help from professionals, it offers still further possibilities.

Another contention of this book and of my own philosophy is that there are times in all of our lives when we are not sufficient unto ourselves. Building a strong family sometimes requires help from someone who sees the family from a distance. Nonetheless, I am quite certain that where there is no severely incapacitating psychopathology on the part of one or both of the parents, it is quite possible for intelligent people to utilize the grid or to utilize any of its principles in order to help them review the dynamics of their family and thus move along on the road to improvement. Building strong families is not the work of children.

I think it's especially important to make it clear that while children have responsibilities, up to a certain point in their lives (which cannot be delineated with any absolute assurance, but which probably means not much before the age of eleven or twelve) children cannot be expected to turn a family around by either their behavior or their misbehavior. Too often parents shuck the burden of building strong families by saying that it's the children's behavior that needs to change, not theirs. This, in fact, may be quite true. But much before eleven or twelve, it is extremely difficult for children to be taught to behave differently toward their parents.

Thus, it is incumbent upon the adult coalition to become the change agent. Building a strong family starts with the parents and infects the children. First the parents must start to consciously make changes in their own behavior. (Note here that I do not say in their psychology or in their basic problems between one another, because I'm not at all sure that it is necessary for parents to go into long and extended explorations of their individual hang-ups in order for them to effect changes in the family structure. But insight into their human behavior does help.)

Changing behavior at home is more likely to result in building a strong family than can all of the philosophy about the psychology of the individual parents. True, we are all products of what we have been and of those who reared us. The things that occur to us in childhood are not irrevocable. But while we are the prisoners of our past, escape from all prisons is possible with a certain amount of daring, ingenuity, and knowledge. So it is with rearing one's family. Constant conscious attempts to change our own behavior as well as the behavior of our spouse and our children will result in a payoff that will be evident in the behavior of all members of the family.

Again, my own experience has led me to conclude that the family problems that most families meet, including the serious one of childhood schizophrenia, are more easily solved by studying the things that people *do* that are hurtful to other people in the family than by studying the psychology of the individuals. One of the differences between man and beast is that man is able to look upon himself and within himself introspectively. This is an urgent experience, one that should always be carried on. But I suggest that there comes a time when all of the fanciful introspection, as accurate as it may be, will end in no significant family interactional differences until one moves from the realm of psychology and philosophy to the pure and simple activity.

An ancient story tells of a young man who came to the rabbi of his small town in Poland and said, "Good rabbi, how can I learn to believe the way you believe?" The rabbi pondered for a moment and then said, "Young man, if you will act the way I act, soon you will learn to believe the way I believe."

One of the valuable aspects of family therapy by an expert is that this therapist should be able, with the constant cooperation and consent of the rest of the family, to delineate those behaviors that go on within the family that feed the pathology of the family. I have talked and counseled that nearly every family is capable of identifying some of the more difficult family behaviors that are standing in the way of the family becoming a therapeutic community. In most cases, there are but a few of these behavior patterns in the repertoire of any of the individuals in that family. For example, if a husband continually compares his wife to someone else's wife, or if a child of sixteen continually says, "No, and you can't make me," or if a wife continually berates a child for every minor infraction of the family's rules without ever consciously seeing the child's positive ways of action, then we may be sure that these behaviors will continue until someone—often an outsider—is able to point to the defective behaviors between the individuals and to suggest ways of changing those behaviors.

There are those who will be upset with this particular point of view. There are those who will say that nothing but deep and continual therapy will effect changes in family pathology. I suggest that it is entirely possible that the afternoon soap operas on television are probably a more potent force for family therapy than all of the combined work of all of the psychiatrists, psychologists, social workers, and therapists in the nation.

I further suggest that it is not out of the realm of possibility at all that neighbors, friends, and relatives have been more positively functioning therapists and have had greater effects upon changing family dysfunction than the combined good works of professionals.

This is *not* to say that the work of professional family therapy is diminished in the slightest. Indeed, it has had and can have significant effects in ameliorating the dysfunction in the family. But its use is limited because its practices are often suspect, often embarrassing, often too costly. Something or someone has to make a difference in a family with trouble.

I have no doubt but that viewing and hearing and watching the progress of family unfold each day on the television screens of America could be far more powerful if it were concentrated upon the more mundane family problems. Indeed, I have suggested that the networks consider using family therapy in the form of afternoon and evening prime-time soap operas where the subject matter would be far more relevant to the lives of the millions who watch. Having recently spent some time in the hospital, I was able to ascertain, by watching one after another of the soap operas, that for the most part the problems evolve upon the exotic in family pathology. For example, infidelity seems to be a major problem and is treated with a great deal of finesse and in a manner that I think could be helpful to people. However, I saw very little of ordinary men and women dealing with the ordinary problems of their children. The soap opera need not be laughed at and should be the last kind of media to be held in scorn by those practicing family therapy, since they should be the first to recognize that despite their expertise and general effectiveness, they simply do not reach any significant portion of the American population.

I think that there ought not to be shame in seeking counsel and help from professionals. I think that in lieu of professional help, the guidance of people whom others emulate as being members of good families may be very, very helpful. I have often said that frequently our neighbors are better for our kids than are ourselves. This simply means that a distance is maintained between neighbors and our children, and ourselves and our neighbors' children, that enables us to see the errors of the ways of our neighbors in a way in which we cannot see those of our own.

Man is continually in the process of removing the splinters from the eyes of others while neglecting the mote in his own. That is the way it is and probably the way it always will be. Building strong families is a lifetime task, a process that never ends. It is not useless, not hopeless. No matter how bad you may feel about your family, the mere will to do better is a beginning. Why not get started?

Learning how to communicate

It is my contention that all learned behavior can be unlearned, and that communication skills are learned skills.

A child may learn as he grows that the silent treatment is one way to get what he wants. He learns that type of behavior if he has observed it in his family.

He learns how to get things off his chest and "level" with someone if he has been lucky enough to watch this process in his family.

He learns how to listen (a very important part of communication) if he has been listened to in his family.

The family is the crucible in which the individual is compounded (and, on occasion, confounded), and communication is taught to the child by the ways in which his family communicates.

Listening is one important form of communication. The way we listen to another person sends a message about what we feel for that person. Troubled families usually complain that no one really listens, and if we have learned not to listen, then we must relearn how to do so.

On the surface, the methods I suggest appear deceptively simple. Anyone can reel them off. Anyone can read them and think that he knows them. But one has not learned unless he has changed his behavior.

First, you must find out who in your family feels that he isn't being listened to. (In finding this out, you must accept his feelings and not argue with him.) Teenagers who are having at-home troubles usually feel unlistened to. When you have identified that person, tell him you want to change your ways of listening; then ask to be told something, and show by your physical and mental attitude that you are listening. It might also be wise to echo or restate some of what you hear so you can check on whether you heard what you thought you heard. If there is some doubt, asking what was meant by what was said goes a long way toward instilling confidence. We often hear what we want to hear. What the ears pick up gets filtered through our entire perceptual system.

If there have been bad feelings in a family, then even this attempt can fail, because while you may be listening, you may also be hearing echoes from past experience. Thus, a mother who assumes her child will lie may be hearing the truth, but once filtered through past experience with that child, the truth becomes a lie no matter how truthful it is.

True dialogue means that each party listens without malice. Impossible after years of noncommunication? Not necessarily. It isn't easy, but it is possible.

So we see that communication isn't all talking; at least half of it is listening. But to what are you listening? First and above all else, a family ought to be a place where it is safe to talk about one's inner space.

Often the first few years of marriage are most difficult

because young couples have fallen into the habit of saying the things one ought to say. One ought to say nice things. One even ought to feel nice things. One ought to say he's sorry. One ought to care. And on and on the list of "ought to's" goes.

There comes a time, however, when the "ought to" behaviors smother some of the real inside-space feelings that we feel we ought to hide. Some of our feelings aren't good ones as we live with others simply because that is the way it is.

Real communication means that while we recognize the value of proprieties, every human being has the need to let some inside feelings flow out. When a woman once cried to her husband, "I wish you were my friend rather than my husband," she was illustrating the importance she placed upon confiding feelings to another in an atmosphere of understanding. You see, "ought to" ideology has as one of its commandments the fact that expressing hostility or fear or worry isn't nice. Well, it isn't very much fun to lay bare deep resentments, but in a family we need a social system in which it is urgent that the home society accepts the hurts as well as the accomplishments.

I know a good mother who always instructs her children to tell her nothing but happy things. If life were just a shimmering bowl of cherry gelatin, this might be just fine; but children have inside hurts, wives have inner feelings of despair, and husbands in their ceaseless providing for needs (substitute moms here too, if they are breadwinners) often have pressures they don't feel they can talk about even to their mates.

Communication in a family must be carried on so that

the folks involved are physically close to one another during it. A phone call isn't communication. Talking over TV isn't communication. Shouting from one room to another isn't communication. People need to set time aside so that they are eyeball to eyeball when it comes to talking times.

With children, communicate at the eye level. Get down to them. With adults, don't be more than two feet apart when you say something you really mean. "Ought to's" can be said anywhere, in any way. Real feelings need to literally be felt and smelled.

Some readers may imagine that I have ruled out any kind of communication that is sweet and tender. When I spoke of "ought to's," it may have sounded as if all human decency was ruled out, so let me make this very clear: We ought to express appreciation for human acts that we too often take for granted. We ought not to be silent about being appreciative. Appreciation builds human feelings.

My dad used to tell me that even a dog wags its tail to tell folks how happy it feels to be with them. The least we can do, since we have the power of speech, is to make certain we tell about the good feelings we do have, whenever we have them. Communicating isn't just the process of spewing forth bad feelings. It is also expressing sincerely our appreciation, praise, and feelings of good will and love.

The real meaning of parent-child communication

Real communication with children is the process of creative listening on the part of parents. It is not benign neglect of what they have to say. It means arranging for times to talk—but even more important, to listen.

Listening doesn't mean believing. Listening well doesn't even mean implicit acceptance of the beliefs of youth. It means caring enough to hear children out. Then they feel real, not like plastic dolls dressed up like children.

In parent-child communication, usually things are reasonably good until the crucial years of fourteen through seventeen. At this time, the effects of adolescence seem to take over, and if parents do not understand what real communication is, a breakdown in the parent-child relationship results. It isn't that there is such a vast difference in ideas (though there often is) between parent and child; it's just that, at about this time, the ideas of the young are often repugnant to elders.

Real communication doesn't mean that parents and children have to see eye-to-eye on matters. It does mean that the parents need to know what the young are thinking.

We often think of communication as exchange. Perhaps it is, in the fullest sense. During adolescence, however, the child usually feels that he has been on the receiving end of messages for fifteen or so years, and it is his turn to do some of the talking. And it is. Remember, the ideas of youth are only that—ideas. While they may sound definitive and authoritative, they are far from being so.

Not long ago I encountered a highly intelligent sixteen-year-old girl who spouted Eastern mysticism as if she had invented it. She was the guru of her age group. A little listening showed that what she thought was really quite tentative, but it sounded absolute. And it is this grim absolutism on the part of the child that makes parents frenzied and frustrated.

Absolutism is the fortress of the insecure, the unsure. Wisdom has always been characterized by something less than a certainty about everything. Indeed, the more uncertain we are, the more tentative our factual knowledge, the closer we are to true maturity. After all, it only takes about forty years of living to realize that society and its whims and fads are fickle. What was avant-garde yesterday is old hat today. What is old stuff today becomes the thing-to-do tomorrow.

Sixteen-year-olds are the most vitriolic dogmatists around. This only means that they are as uncertain as they sound certain. When parents respond with disgust, horror, and disdain to their ideas, teenagers sense that this is a way they can get their parents' goat.

Real communication should mean that parents force themselves to listen to the "revelations" of the young. It would be better if the listening were not forced, but were the sort of attentive interest accorded anyone who asks for a forum. It is a serious breach of ethics to show discourtesy to those who are younger than we and who have newly discovered art, mysticism, or the value of wholewheat bread. Growing up is the process of uncovering anew that which has already been known.

Young people are not really trying to convert their parents so much as they are wanting to test their "new" discoveries. As exasperating as it may be to hear a philosophy preached that you have already resolved, your children need your full attention as they seek to try out the variety of ideas that have tantalized man forever.

Listening with the third ear

Who hasn't had the feeling of talking to someone and being heard but not listened to?

Wherever many people gather—conventions, meetings, large parties—there is a lot of talking going on as people gather in knots to exchange ideas. Perhaps *exchange* isn't the most appropriate word here. *Hear* ideas would be better.

Too often this is precisely what happens at home. Children report that it is a frequent occurrence at school, too. Listening to a child is an art that requires some discipline on the part of an adult. There are a few simple things parents need to practice.

First, when a child indicates that he wants to say something to you, and it is appropriate to hear and listen to what he has to say (that is, he hasn't violated some elementary rules of etiquette), stop what you are doing and give him your full attention. If the child is a preschooler, get down to where he is or bring him up to where you are, and then let him talk. By looking right at the child, you encourage him to continue. A child requires the undivided attention of the adults in his world. At all times? Of course not. But when he indicates that he has something to say, and you have indicated that you would be willing to listen to it, then he deserves undivided attention.

Second, with the very young child it might be well to listen with one arm around him so that you form sort of a "cuddle" right then and there. A cuddle is a huddle for folks who haven't football equipment. By doing this you sort of shut out the rest of the world, the family, and the neighborhood, and the two of you are talking with no outside, busy world intervening.

Third, in order to prove that you really are listening, it is important that you answer all questions as they are asked. If it isn't that kind of conversation, then you need to nod often, rephrase what you think you have heard, and then encourage the child to express himself fully. There may even be a time when you will want to try a summation of what you heard and, if the world is pressing, learn how to end the conversation with politeness and discretion.

In my home I frequently indicate my office door to my children, and in we go to do some listening. And here is where the "listening with the third ear" comes in.

In all children, no matter what age, there is much that they say when they either say nothing or when they say what they do not mean to say. The kind of listening that reads between the lines and that has sensitive antennae up all the time will enable you to hear what is said, especially with adolescents. It will then help you to rephrase what you hear, or interpret, to see if you can focus on what the child may have wished to say but simply couldn't.

In our house a few weeks ago, my teenage daughter

seemed to be wandering around sighing under her breath just loud enough for someone to hear. This is not language in its fullest sense, but it is what are called covert signals. That is, she had something on her mind, but for some reason she wasn't able to find anyone to tell it to. The long sighs, the woebegone look, and the wistfulness all sent clear messages to alert parents who finally decided to take the opportunity to have a private moment together. And then it flowed.

I have found that innocent questions often betray deep feelings about matters that cannot be asked directly. I recollect one from a child who asked her father if it was okay to disappoint someone even if you liked them. In this case, there was no long recitation of a story, just the question, which, if parents were really listening with that third ear, could tell them that there was more to the question than the ear had heard.

When we listen with the third ear, we open our awareness to the feelings of others who sometimes cannot bring their feelings to the "speaking out" level of consciousness.

I have always appreciated friends who have been perceptive enough to know when I really needed them even if my verbal messages didn't communicate that need. When adults have developed this acute sensitivity to unspoken needs, whether of children or of adults, the world becomes a better place in which to live.

Touching isn't taboo

Want to try something different the next time you decide to have a heart-to-heart talk with one of your children?

Try touching. Put your arm around him; touch his arm; show that he is more than just an errant youth.

An angry mother once shouted at me that the professional child watchers keep screaming at harried mothers and fathers about communicating with their children, but no one ever really tells them how to communicate.

One way is to let your humanness out in the form of touching. Aha, you may be saying to yourself as you read this, Landau has fallen for the Esalen communication business—come as you are, etc. No, I am really convinced that a strict hands-off policy between parents and children, husbands and wives is too antiseptic to foster real communication.

Harry Harlow's famous work with baby monkeys showed clearly that no matter what type of substitute-mother was offered a baby monkey, the one preferred was the one that felt good, in this case a terrycloth-covered monkey. Harlow called this contact comfort. Here is what he said about those observations:

"We were not surprised to discover that contact comfort was an important basic affectional or love variable, but we did not expect it to overshadow so completely the variable of nursing; indeed, the disparity is so great as to suggest that the primary function of nursing as an affectional variable is that of insuring frequent and intimate body contact of the infant with the mother."

In the early 1900s many infant deaths were due to a baffling disease, marasmus, which literally means "wasting away." It was found that children either at home or hospitalized who received little or no physical handling started to deteriorate so that they actually lost the functioning of most of their vital activities.

Today we are quite sure that bad homes are better than most institutions. At least in a bad home you might get slapped and tossed about, which is better than being in a situation where the staff is too busy to do even these kinds of negative things.

As we saw pictures of our returning POWs being united with their families after years of separation, I only noted one case in which a soldier greeted his son with only a handshake. I hope this was followed up by some real hugging and holding.

Somehow children and animals sense when we really care. I am not suggesting that teachers and parents continually fondle their children. I *am* pleading for appropriate touching so that those we touch realize that physical attention is part of the attempt to bridge the communication gap.

When we touch the people we love, sometimes gently on the shoulder, the elbow, or arm, sometimes—with those we know better—on the back of the neck, even the friendly side kick, we tell them we accept them. This kind of touching is clearly the nonsexual type and is not to be misunderstood as anything but a further attempt to communicate in a non-verbal way.

The family interaction grid

Some months ago I was asked to work with a group of parents, all of whom had married for the second or third time and were rearing the children of another mother or father. We called the course "Parenting the Stepchild," although I never was happy about that title.

Of all the things in human growth and development I am *not* sure about, of one thing I am certain. That is, rearing children is touchy enough when they are really yours, your flesh and blood as it were. But when it comes to rearing someone else's, especially if that someone else is now living with you, there is plenty of room for heartache.

The Division of Family Services of Utah wanted some of its social workers to learn how to deal with these problems, and I suddenly had two different types of individuals to satisfy: (1) parents who were presently living under these special circumstances, and (2) professionals who needed to learn how to help others deal with this problem.

And so one evening I sat down to try to devise a dramatic and graphic way of satisfying the needs of both groups. Out of sheer desperation I developed the Family

Interaction Grid (FIG), which is nothing more than a very complicated, giant-sized chart that often runs ten to fifteen feet in length and three to four feet in height.

If you understand what I am saying, you should be able to do it for yourself. However, a word or two of caution—if you follow my directions, you will not necessarily solve your family's problems. This is a diagnostic* technique and, just like the physician whose stethoscope may detect a murmur of the heart but who is not able to cure that murmur, all that this grid can do is lay out before you what is going on in your family. Also, you need not be a reconstituted family in order to utilize this instrument.

First, draw two fairly large boxes, say one foot wide by two feet tall, and label these Mom and Dad or Harvey and Judy. Under these two, place the appropriate number of equal-shaped boxes, each representing one of the children of the family.

If you happen to be remarried and living with your spouse's children, your own, and perhaps children who belong to both of you, draw these boxes so that the children that were yours in the first instance are connected to you by dark lines. Better still, draw these boxes so that they are directly to the side of your box and away from your spouse's box. Thus, if you have a remarried situation, your children will be "closer" to you, and your husband's children will be drawn so that they cluster near him and off to his side.

Next, in each of the boxes—yours, your spouse's, and one for each of your children—list very briefly the facts of

---

*I have been reminded by a practicing psychiatrist that the grid is also therapeutic.

the present state of the family and then, also succinctly, the feelings each of you have about the problems in your family.

If all of this is done separately and then with everyone present, what should emerge is a grid that rather vividly and accurately outlines the facts and feelings about your family at the present time.

Finally, it is up to everyone concerned to discuss one another's grid, then to agree upon the three most difficult problems encountered in the family. If possible, the most upsetting problem should be identified and circled with a red line.

When there is unanimous agreement about the most serious problem, you have successfully completed a Family Interaction Grid. What you do with it from this point on is important. You can choose to ignore it or you can use it for a basis of further discussion in the family so that the red-lined problem(s) start to get solved. If the problem looks serious enough, there is wisdom in seeking help from a qualified family counselor, psychologist, or physician. Since this is primarily a diagnostic tool, it is limited in its therapeutic effect.

Should you be curious about the further steps likely to be taken by a therapist who might use the technique or another similar one, here is what may happen. Two further techniques have been devised—the PIP or Professional's Intervention Plan, in which the professional will devise either his own or the family's next moves to conquer their problems, and an Individual's Commitment Plan (ICP), which are the specific steps all family members will take as they jointly try to ameliorate the more serious family problems.

When families share their problems with one another

instead of smouldering, and when families attempt, with professional help, to alter their personal behavior so that the aggravating circumstances are lessened, there is hope for today's family.

Every family needs rules

If you want to find out what makes your family tick, there are some important activities you need to check and double check.

First, a family is a social system. Like any system in which folks need to do more than simply survive, the family needs to have rules that are clear, fair, and in keeping with its general code of behavior. There are implicit rules or those which are unspoken, yet are a vital part of the family life. For example, if a meal does not begin until father is at the table, and if this has always been so, then we may designate this an implicit rule.

On the other hand, if it has been explicitly stated that no meal starts without some discussion of world or family affairs, we would call this an overt rule. In fact, it does not matter whether the rules are simply understood or are carefully spelled out. The important consideration is that there are rules.

Some psychologists feel that covert rules are unfair. That is, these rules suddenly emerge in response to a situation that develops in the family for which there has been no precedent. I see no particular evil here, since it takes new rules to deal with new situations. This is no time for hairsplitting. Rules in a family keep order and prevent anarchy. Rules develop in response to needs.

What *is* unfair is to find that there are rules that everyone thought were clear and which, in fact, are not. Thus, when a child brings a friend home to sleep after everyone else has gone to bed and then discovers in the morning that he has broken a rule, one that he did not know existed, the family has grounds for trouble.

Try this little experiment. First, sit down with the family and try to determine what the rules of the house are. It might be well to spend enough time so that many areas of existence are discussed. Where it is doubtful that there are rules, it might be well as a family to discuss the rule that should apply.

In a sense, a no-rules house is a trap for the young, who cannot help but err as they meet the various life conditions in any home. Is it possible that many adults also like life with no rules so that they can carry on a continual skirmish with the young who cannot, under these conditions, know right from wrong?

The rules assessment described above may uncover a host of rules that are outmoded. They may, for example, have been excellent four years ago when there were no teenagers in the house, but how do they fit now? For example, a rule concerning late hours for a child in the sixth grade may be highly inappropriate for a tenth grader with special events to attend in high school. New rules have to be developed to meet an older family. This process of discovering which rules operate and which do not is in and of itself a healthful exercise, for if new rules need to be developed, the children can share in their formulation, thus giving them a share in the running of their own lives. One axiom of a great democracy is that folks who are affected by decisions ought to have a share in the formulation of those decisions.

Anxiety is a common enough phenomenon among growing people, and homes need to have rules that allow for the discussion and resolution of anxieties and "forbidden" subjects either originating in or outside the home. There ought to be ways for children and adults to signal others that they have an anxiety to share. A good home is a place where one feels free to express hurt or fear or worry.

If the rules preclude this possibility, such as one that says no one is to bring up things that upset others, then children bottle up hurts and obey the rules while grimly slogging their way through a life of silence.

What kept 200 adolescents from trouble?

In 1967 and 1970 James A. Knight reported his now famous study of two hundred highly successful college students who were asked what in their background or life experience had kept them on an effective and goal-oriented path. (See "Resisting the Call of the Cave," *Medical Insight,* 2:66–77.)

The students identified family as the most important motivational factor in their lives. They went even further and mentioned specific and particular values and characteristics that their families promulgated.

The values explicitly taught (or caught) in these families included (1) firmness, (2) direction without dictation, (3) rules that make sense, (4) high expectations of all family members, (5) mutual trust and respect, and (6) the children always knew that "God didn't make no junk," that they were somebody. Let's talk about the first two of these values.

First, *firmness.* What does it mean? What is the operational definition of the term (that is, what does a parent *do* to be firm)? It means that parental values about any and all matters prevail. They are explicitly stated and explained, and adherence is expected. Caution: a parent should be neither too rigid nor too permissive. Draw back when it's wise to do so. Don't leave most of your children's decisions to them. Help them talk and work their way through problems.

And second, *direction without dictation:* Putting this theory into practice means that in all facets of life the children sense the pervading direction that emanates from their parents ("we feel," "we believe," "our experience has been") as they continually consult with one another from toddlerhood to adolescence. Naturally, this consultation diminishes as the children grow older, yet achieve high peaks even during late adolescence. It means that the family rarely orders behavior without precedent and explanation. Only in times of mental danger should it be necessary to say, "Do it, and do it *now* and without ifs, ands, buts, or ors."

If parents normally direct rather than dictate, the few times that dictating is in order will be harmless.

What kind of family discipline?

To punish or not to punish? To rant and rave or not to rant and rave? Ground him? Slap him? Forbid him?

These are questions that have faced parents in all ages.

If there were clear-cut, perfect answers, the questions would not persist. How a parent behaves in the face of the defiance of children, or before their misbehavior, depends greatly upon the family philosophy.

In general, there are three types of parental behavior, each rather readily identifiable, each signifying the type of response the parent will make to the general behavior of his children.

First there is the *authoritarian* parent; next, the *authoritative* parental response to misbehavior; and finally, the *permissive* parent.

Each of these parental responses is unique, rather clearly definable, and sure to lead to a certain type of general family atmosphere. You might enjoy using this yardstick to classify your own family behavior. If the shoe fits, wear it. If you don't like the way the shoe feels, consult with your spouse about making some changes. If you decide to change, remember: Change is possible, but painful.

The authoritarian parent: This type of parent exhibits behavior that either very closely approximates what he lived through himself or behavior that contrasts sharply with the way he was reared.

Erik Erikson in his classic volume *Childhood and Society* (W. W. Norton, 1950) describes one pattern of German fatherhood which, while not intended to define all German families, does reflect my own thought about the authoritarian family. He says that when this type of father comes home from work, "even the walls seem to pull themselves together." Everyone behaves differently when he is home. The mother fulfills the father's whims unhesitatingly; the children are not playful. He speaks to his wife as he does to his children. Mother keeps transgressions of the children from father. Father's word is law. There is no argument after he has spoken. He is not cold or harsh; he is simply distant and commanding.

While few may fit this stereotype exactly, it nonetheless delineates an extreme type of individual who is more likely to create an atmosphere of fear and repression in the home than love and understanding.

The authoritative parent: A decision needs to be made soon. Will the children accompany their parents to grandma, or may they stay home and finish schoolwork and chores? What will the authoritarian parent do, based upon what I described above?

If you conclude that he says, "The children will stay home and do their work. We will call them when we get to my mother's," then you have understood authoritarianism.

If, however, father consults the children, listens to their plans and reasoning, and then proposes a plan consistent with their ideas, you may assume that he is *authoritative*. He may make the final decision but not without reasonable consultation.

The authoritative parent tries to direct his child's activities, but in a rational manner. The rules and regulations in the house spring from pertinent issues. The parent uses reason but does not shun the use of power.

The permissive parent: This parent is nonpunitive. He accepts the child's impulses as being natural and desirable. Children are not only listened to; they are also held to no responsibility, either in or around the house. The adult doesn't feel that he has any right to shape a child's behavior. The parent is a resource and nothing more. Orderly behavior is secondary to freedom and creativity.

Dr. Diane Baumrind, in a study at the Parental Authority Research Project in Berkeley, California, found that punishment does not always have negative side effects. The study found that the least hostile and rebellious children came from homes in which high demands were made by parents who were firmly in control. These parents practiced rational, warm, and issue-oriented authority. Therefore, they were authoritative-type parents.

Dr. Baumrind's other conclusions were that permissiveness does not breed conscience while either authoritarian or permissive attitudes create angry attacks by the children. In short, both excessive permissiveness (because it provides no structure or guidelines) and excessive controls (because they permit no independent action) lead to neurotic insecurity and aimlessness.

Freedom isn't license

In A. S. Neill's book *Summerhill* (New York: Hart Publishing Co., 1960), the author tells the story of his school in London, where the theory that children thrive best in an atmosphere of freedom, rather than repression, was put into practice. There were many who interpreted his story to mean that there should be no limits placed on children.

When Neill discovered he had been misread, he published another book entitled *Freedom—Not License* (New York, Hart Publishing Co., 1966). In this book, he more than once indicated his utter horror at the children of various friends and acquaintances of his. In one case a child felt obligated to dominate the conversation originated by the adults. Neill was so upset that he asked the child to be quiet and told him that he wasn't invited to participate in the discussion. Neill thought it incredulous that a parent would silently permit a child to take over an adult conservation. This wasn't freedom—it was license.

One of Neill's most important points can be wisely used by all parents. Freedom is vital. To be allowed to be a child is decent and humane. To allow and even encourage freedom is good. But the difference between freedom and license is larger than one would suppose from a simple reading of Neill.

It is true that children can wear and say and do about what they please, providing their dress, words, and actions do not infringe upon the rights of others who share the ecosystem.

This general principle holds true in other cases. One is, and by rights ought to be, free to smoke or not to smoke; to drink or not to drink; to cavort or not to cavort. No one really has the right to impose his standards on another. But if the behavior of one party is deleterious to the health and welfare of anyone else, then it is the offending party who must cease and desist.

License implies behavior that steps on the rights of anyone else, and this is exactly how to describe it even to very small children. We curtail their freedom when their behavior, in the judgment of the parent, is likely to trample upon the rights of another.

Neill cites the example of having a conversation with a visitor in a room in which there was a television set. One of the Summerhill children came in and turned on the set and proceeded to watch. Neill quickly stepped to the set, snapped it off, and said, "Look here, young man, we were conversing. You intruded, and though you did not enter into our conversation, you were forcing us to either move or shout. You have just stepped over the line of propriety. Out you go. Your freedom may not mean my discomfort."

Children have certain freedoms too. The "right" to beat your child because he is yours is not right at all. It is license. Every child who is beaten, not spatted, loses his freedom to live without harm being done to his person. Imagine the inequity of a 130-pounder pummeling a 28-pounder. Even the boxing world sets limits on who can fight whom based upon weight.

No human has the license to trample upon the person or feelings of another. Someone has wisely said that "your freedom ends where my nose begins." In the physical realm this is easy to understand; in the world of the emotions it isn't so simple. No person has the right to belittle another or emotionally cut him down. Too often boss and worker relationships are based upon the feeling of either one of the parties that it is his right to bully the other by virtue of his position.

So, allow every bit of freedom to the developing child consistent with the principle of that freedom being his until he places another's in jeopardy or endangers himself. The latter is especially important with very young children, since they most often do not understand where safety ends and danger begins. Freedom, yes; license, never!

In families self-esteem is vital

One of the great figures in the field of family therapy is Virginia Satir, who wrote *Conjoint Family Therapy*, a manual for professionals who deal with family problems.

In her latest book, called *People Making* (Science and Behavior Books, 1972), Mrs. Satir calls the family a factory where the adults are the people-makers. Children do not shape a family; adults do. This is a very important concept. Too many people do not realize that it is the adult persons in a family who set the tone for the entire group living together. Only immature adults blame their children for family disharmony.

I like what Mrs. Satir says about what a human being is like: "He is a person who understands, values, and develops his body, finding it beautiful and useful; a person who is willing to take risks, to be creative, to manifest competence, to change when the situation calls for it, and to find ways to accommodate to what is new and different, keeping that part of the old that is still useful and discarding what is not.

"When you add all of this up, you have a physically

healthy, mentally alert, feeling, loving, playful, authentic, creative, productive human being."

I'm sure that as you run down this list of ideal attributes, you do just what any of us would—mentally tick off the weak and strong places in your own personality.

A family is composed of a certain number of unique individuals who have joined together to perpetuate the race. Hopefully, their journey together will be healthy and productive. It cannot be such if the two adults who head that family are not somewhere near the profile of the truly functioning human being just mentioned.

When the family becomes a unit, it starts to function as a body. It sets up a variety of systems within its structure. These are readily observable and assessable by a competent counselor and even by members of the family itself, as they comprehend the meaning of each aspect of family life.

In troubled families, many of the members—especially the adults—have deep feelings of personal worthlessness. Troubled families have few rules about how they should feel and act toward one another. Finally, the troubled family has distinct problems linking itself to institutions outside the family.

Self-worth is one of four aspects of family life that must be operating well in order to produce a healthy unit. In order for a family to function happily, its principal adults must feel they are worthwhile individuals.

You can ask yourself these simple questions: Am I on earth to make the world a better place, and is it a better place because I am here? This does not mean that you need to be a headliner or a TV star. If you have made yourself significant to others in even the smallest way and you feel good about that, then you have self-worth. Do you accept the feelings you have inside of you as being real and human? Then you value yourself.

Everyone gets low on occasion, down in the mouth, fed up. If you don't, something is mighty wrong with you. If you are rearing a family and you are an ordinary mother with all of the 4 P.M. problems, you are sometimes bound to be willing to trade the diapers and meals for a brief moment skydiving or playing three slot machines at once.

The vital person, however, treats these things as being temporary conditions and little else.

People who are low on themselves expect to be kicked around in the world, expect to be cheated and deprecated. Their defense is to become cynical and bitter. They naturally become fearful, and their fear blinds and binds them. They look ahead and won't take any road because they are certain it ends up the creek. And so it goes, and so a person with continual low self-esteem infects the rest of the family, and another generation is doomed.

You might look at yourself now. When did you last feel great about the world? Can you recollect the moment? Savor it; try to call it back. It feels very good. It should, because it is one of the most important feelings in the world.

If you can't remember any good feelings, it is time you started to join in with others, anywhere—church, gardening course, high school refresher class—it matters not where, just so long as you force yourself out to interact with others who may find in you the value you have lost.

Never forget the bedside prayer of the little girl who said, "I know God didn't make no junk." He didn't and you have to believe it and start to act like it.

Making good behavior pay

At age eleven Jack seldom picked up his saxophone. He played quite well but was showing no improvement. His parents felt their efforts were not paying off. Another few months on this plateau and Jack would probably give up the instrument. What usually happens between parent and child at this time is the age-old battle that ends in bitterness, frustration, and finally capitulation by one or the other.

If the child wins, the rented instrument is returned and little is said except for occasional verbal exchanges in which the parents (usually mother) clearly indicate that they have done their part—the rest is up to the child.

If the parent wins, the child continues his music lessons with two possible kinds of results. First, if he perseveres through gritted teeth, he may one day become proficient and thankful for his mother's adamancy. Second, he may carry on in quiet desperation, vowing silently to take his revenge somehow.

There are ways, however, to avoid a parent-child battle over practicing. The first thing Jack's family could do is to consciously (this means not accidentally) look for things to praise when Jack practices. Dad could make a casual but intentional reference to a tune he remembered in "the good old days." The boy's sister could point our her delight at the prospect that one day they could play a duet. His usually silent older brother could even go out of his way to comment upon the kid brother's talent.

To further strengthen the verbal approval already given by the family, mother could suggest that he practice during the time he usually helps with the dinner dishes. We might call this an offer he couldn't refuse.

In a week or so the family could plan an outing to a performance of a group whose lead man plays a "hot" sax.

When Jack starts to enjoy his family's attention, his dad could purchase a new saxophone to replace the rental instrument. By this time, Jack will probably be really enthusiastic about his lessons and his practicing.

Finally, the band at school might invite Jack to join. With this added honor he would no longer need the artificial family support, and his interest in practicing and improving would be intrinsic.

Sure, this is a contrived, pre-planned assault and thus somewhat artificial, but nonetheless, it is really the way folks ought to respond to one another's endeavors. In most families, if someone practices, either nothing is said or what is said tends to be deprecatory.

Of great importance in Jack's progress is the enthusiastic approval of his entire family. Too often we take for granted acceptable behavior and let it pass unnoticed. As families, we need to verbally revel in the accomplishments of each other even if they appear to be trivial. Remember, the behavior to which we pay attention will likely be repeated.

Be positive for a change

"We've been married fourteen years, and in all that time he's never picked up his socks and underwear and put them in the hamper," moaned the trim, thirtyish lady in the first row of a lecture hall in El Paso, Texas.

This was in response to my inquiry about an annoying behavior someone wishes to change in her spouse.

"And what have you done about it in the last fourteen years?"

"Done about it? Dr. Landau, I've just learned to live with it."

"Then you don't care to change his behavior?" I smilingly asked.

"Oh, no, I do. It's just that after so many years of raging, pleading, crying, and nagging every single morning of our married lives, I've sort of resigned myself to it."

After trying my few simple suggestions, this lady later excitedly reported that in three days her husband had, for the first time in years, chucked his socks and underwear into the hamper.

What did I tell her to do? I told her to stop reminding

her husband about what he didn't do—after all, in fourteen years that kind of behavior didn't change him—and to start a planned strategy that would have her list all of the things he did do that she approved of and then to systematically, regularly, and frequently comment about these. In other words, I asked her to pay little or no attention to the behavior she disapproved of and to pay liberal attention to the behavior she liked. Presto! A persistent source of conflict disappeared.

There is no miracle-cure for ameliorating most human conditions. If something appears to be miraculous, it too often has negative side effects. No one-shot injection of positive response is likely to heal fourteen years of constant nagging.

You might say that I lucked out. Her careful verbal attention to her husband's exemplary behavior—covering up the kids in their beds at night, turning off the air conditioning, mixing the orange juice, letting out the cat, starting the sprinklers, etc.—did the trick. In just a few days he started to feel appreciated, and so he began to remember to do the one little thing his wife never let him forget.

Let's change the scene: Now this same mother is home with her two preschool-age children every day. After breakfast each morning the kids dutifully go in to watch "Romper Room" or its equivalent on TV, and mom starts her morning routine. For the past year or so it has been an erratic, continually interrupted routine. About every eight minutes or so, some loud scream from one of the children sends mother on a mad dash to stop the screaming and mayhem.

Is there a way to at least minimize the fighting, the arguing, the childish behavior of the children? Of course not. No one can hurry up maturation. We can't make a frog out of a tadpole by cutting off its tail. We can, however, decrease the number of times mom rushes into the TV room. By applying the same ideas noted earlier, we can decrease the fighting behavior of the children.

Remember the correct principle: We try to ignore behavior we wish to extinguish (fighting, arguing, etc.), and we pay a great deal of verbal attention to behavior we wish to have repeated.

Instead of mother thanking her lucky stars when the children are quiet and attentive, she should, because she wants that lovely behavior to be repeated, go into the room and tell the children how pleased she is, how sweet they are, maybe bring in a treat, and then exit. If she pays enough attention to the good behavior, the children will soon learn that that kind of behavior brings mother in with compliments, cookies, and smiles. They like that! If she persists in just responding to their negative behavior, they learn to act up in order to bring mom in.

We change human behavior best when we verbally approve of positive actions. If our life experience is one of overwhelming approval for our actions, we feel good about ourselves and our lives. If our actions bring only negative responses from those with whom we live, there is little reason or incentive to change.

Give
praise
for
kindness

Until your little boy looks you in the eye and asks why the world is so full of war and hate, until you feel his fear for himself at the prospect of slogging through some far-away jungle, you can't begin to comprehend my cautiousness as I start to write this chapter.

In the New York *Times* magazine section of March 18, 1973, Dr. Kenneth Clark, professor of psychology at the City College of New York, the man whose data on the hurt inflicted upon black children through school desegregation moved the Supreme Court to its landmark 1954 school desegregation decision, tells his interviewer that he believes he has the answer to the world's persistent inequities.

In this unusual article in which he is asked to reflect upon the progress his people have made since 1954, Dr. Clark refers to an article by Bertrand Russell in which the philosopher is asked whether there is a solution to the fundamental problem of human cruelty and conflict. Russell, claiming some embarrassment at his simple, unsophisticated answers, said, "If we could find some way in which human beings could have kindness as the essence of their relationship with their fellow human beings, this would be the answer."

An intriguing problem is raised for those of us either contemplating or rearing families. An equally challenging dare is aimed at those who lead our schools. If Russell's answer is so simple, why couldn't we reorder the priorities assigned to growth and development of our children at home or at school? Our goal is kindness, isn't it? Suppose we decide to rarely emphasize or reinforce anything at home or at school *but* kindness. Let's see how it might work. If you allow me this flight of fancy, let's see where it takes us.

When Jimmy gets up in the morning and makes his bed, we say nothing. If he comes in to breakfast on time, we make no comment. If he does his homework chores or vacuums his room, we simply take it for granted. If he gets A's on his report card, we ignore it; if he makes the varsity team, we simply shrug our shoulders.

Remember, our objective is to make kindness the most valued human experience. So—

If Jimmy gets his sister up so she won't be late, we loudly approve. If he sets the table for the family, we really whoop it up. If he helps a friend or his sister with their homework, we act as if it is the greatest triumph of the day. If he's kind to anyone, we make much of it.

In other words, from infancy up we will only reward those behaviors that exhibit human kindness.

Dr. Jerome Kagan of Harvard University recently wrote that in grades 1 through 3 we should only give good marks for altruistic behavior. Just as once we graded deportment or conduct, just as now we give A's for academic achievement, he suggests that in order to alter significantly the value systems of our six-, seven-, and eight-year-olds, we only give

A's for being decent and fair and attach less value to outstanding scholastic attainment. By the time the child reaches the age of six, if we haven't thoroughly stressed the old-new value of kindness, it is nearly too late.

As a nation we tend to venerate the intellect, the affluent, the brave, and the athletic. And so, early in a child's life, we point the way to these four pillars of success and give great approval to success in any or all of these endeavors. As a result, we reap what we have sown—a world more interested in victory, honor, and riches than in kindness, concern, and the nurturing of humans.

The world is full of war and hate because the people have venerated false gods. The comic strip character Pogo said it nicely: "We have met the enemy and he is us."

Tradition

Who can forget Tevye in *Fiddler on the Roof* as he sang the great song "Tradition"? Tradition is the cement that binds the human family into a solid, forward-looking union. Count Alfred Korzybski, the father of the science of semantics, once said that the one thing which differentiates homo sapiens from every other species is that humans are time-binding. They are able to create through their linguistic capacity a bridge between all the men who have ever lived before and the men who are living presently. They are, in fact, able to transmit their heritage, their traditions.

In Antoine de St. Exupery's delicate book *The Little Prince* there is a discussion of rites. It is explained that rites help folks establish ties.

One way the modern family can establish ties is to develop traditions that remind the children and parents that they are unique as a family group and, at the same time, that they are joined to the human family by traditions they share with many others. One example of the latter is the simple matter of observing holidays that are also observed by millions of others. Apparently apple pie and milk shakes are becoming a tradition, if not already so, in America. Witness the returning POWs who said that they were almost kept alive by dreams of this delight.

Religious rites are important in preserving traditional family values because they are not only shared by so many others, but are also adapted by each family to suit its particular whims and needs. Some folks, in an attempt to be "with it," have cut religious rites from their family experience. However, these observances are time-binding and fulfill the human desire to be a part of a greater body.

I will never forget the young man who, hearing of a couple contemplating a marriage between two different religions, said, "I only wish that my parents had made me something instead of nothing. At least I would have known what to revolt from. Now I have nothing to fight but myself."

When I recently asked a group of drug addicts what it is they most remember about their families, not one could point to a tradition they considered a binding agent in their early lives. Give your children some solid framework, some structure that will help them to identify themselves with a substantial number of other human beings.

Each family can develop traditions within the unit, such as meals composed of the family's favorite foods, or vacation spots and recreation places regularly visited. A tradition as simple as attending a certain concert annually on the same day of the year or watching *The Wizard of Oz* together is a good start.

In our frantic, modern rush for providing varied experiences for children, we have too often forgotten that the monotony of tradition may not be so monotonous after all.

Why not assess your family today to make sure you are sharing traditional experiences?

Secret
survival
in
society

A healthy family does not—cannot—exist in vacuum. It cannot exist without linking itself with a variety of outside-the-family institutions. The interdependency of the family upon the society that surrounds it is evident.

A completely idiosyncratic family—that is, one that ignores the schools, churches, and community structure, such as law and government—develops introversion in its members that is inimical to good growth. However, a family may reject all of the values of all of the institutions that surround it and survive quite well, if that family is linked somehow to an institution that shares its peculiar nature.

Thus, for example, when a family doesn't share the religious ideology of the community in which it exists, a severe sickness can attack that family unless it is linked rather purposely with an institution that reinforces its differences.

The same is true for political ideology. A person may be vastly different in this realm from those around him, but in order to prevent paranoia from setting in, there must be an attachment or linkage to someone, somewhere, that supports an island of difference in a sea of sameness.

Healthy families develop a wide variety of ties with a varied spectrum of outside institutions. This brings into the family circle the diverse influences of different people, all of whom contribute to the personality growth of the individual members of the family.

Specifically, the family that goes to a church together still needs, for the full flowering of its members, affiliation with other groups, such as a political group or a special interest group (Sierra Club, Rock Hound Club, Lions Club, Travel Group, Boating Association, etc.). The vast individual differences in a family almost cry out for diversity. The antithesis of this occurs when outside institutions envelop the family so completely that the family is suffocated by a single influence.

One of the functions of parents is to assess their children's linkage patterns and see that their brilliant individuality is not eclipsed. In other words, the culture of each family is distinctive. It is the result of the "mix," genetic and social, that gives character to the family.

The family culture needs to develop continually so that it becomes a deeply felt and shared life that at its best reaches out in an attempt to link up with surrounding organizations. It must not be the reverse. If institutions become the family, if they are the *only* role models in the lives of the children, the intimate human associations are supplanted by the "corporate" substitute.

Though the Israeli kibbutz nursery nearly became that corporate substitute, it was decided, and wisely, that children should spend not only sleeping hours at home, but also two full hours daily with their parents.

A link, then, is not a weld. A weld eventually makes indistinguishable the two different pieces fused. The links between families and institutions are of a different nature. In a linkage there is freedom to break the link when and where necessary and to attach to other institutions without severe rupture. Thus a healthy family understands that its linkage to institutions is a healthy way of affiliating with nonfamily enterprises, which, because of their influence, make life more satisfying.

THE CHILDREN

The purpose of all good family life is to provide for a good child's life. It has been said that "the child is father to the man." This simply means that the experiences that men have as children shape what they are like when they become men. It is generally acknowledged that the kind of father a child becomes is often determined by the kind of father with whom he has been brought up in his family. Therefore, the child in the family will become very much like the man in his own family. (The use of the male term here is simply grammatic; the same is true for the girl, of course.)

I am impressed with the professional literature that studies the quality of family life as it affects the child at home, at school, and with his peer group. Allow me to cite a recent instance that came to my attention. In this particular family, which included a number of adopted children, the father has always had a difficult time really caring for one particular child. His difficulty has been compounded by the fact that the child has always had the feeling of not belonging. One is unable to determine whether or not the child's feeling is part of his genetic makeup or if his father's feelings have been communicated to him from the time that he was adopted. I suspect both are true, with the latter being more important. It took a number of years for the parents to realize that they simply did not feel about this child as they did about the others, even though most of the others were adopted.

The ability to face oneself and determine how one feels about the various members of the family is an extraordinarily difficult process. But the life of this particular child has been and will be continually affected by the tone of feeling in that family and by the admission of at least one of the parents that his emotional response to the child has always been minimal. It's the same old problem of what comes first, the chicken or the egg. Was the child difficult to start with, and so his parents responded to his difficulty with petulance and disappointment, and thus caused him to feel worse about his original difficulty?

In the absence of real knowledge about the role of genetics in human development, it is important to try to assess the problems in any family on the basis of the fact that the family has some responsibility for the well-being of the child. In fact, it may be true that the largest percentage of a human being's responses to his environment are related to his genetic makeup. At the present time, it is impossible to say this. Therefore, we must deal with what we can—namely, the conditions of living that surround each individual in the family.

A mother once told me that she felt she was a wonderful mother until her children became six or seven. She freely admitted that she did well when she was in complete control, but the moment the children started to walk and talk and behave on their own, she felt entirely inadequate and found most of their behavior to be below par.

It isn't unusual for people to find difficulties with their children increasing as the children grow older. My own mother has said, "Little children, little problems; big children, big problems." This doesn't mean that there's any great fault in a parent who observes this in his or her behavior. But the response of the adult who regrets the growing-up process, or who at least can't cope with the process of the child's separating, both emotionally and physically, from his parents, is one that has to be faced. It does not mean that the parent is emotionally ill or not able to survive the family experience. It simply means that the parent finds life more difficult with older children than with younger children. Nevertheless, the life of the family must go on despite the feelings of the parents with regard to the ages of their children.

Paraphrasing our earlier statement, we may say, "The family is father to the child." The child is in the family; the family is in the child. The mutuality of influence is evident. What is not evident is the amount of the child's influence on the family or of the family's influence upon the child. Again, in the absence of scientific knowledge, it would be wise to assume that the things that happen in a family have greater import on the development of the child than the child has upon the development of the family.

The child is very much *in* the family. The interactions between children and children, between parents and children, and between the parents themselves—all play a major role in the developing child's personality. The normal course of development is for the child, when very young, to be very much in the family and, as he grows older, to gradually move further and further away from it. For both the child and his parents, this is difficult. For some children, it is extremely difficult; for some parents, it is likewise extremely difficult. Parents who are emotionally immature may find that the separation of the child from the family, which eventually results in marriage and the child's starting to develop his own family, is very traumatic. The healthier the parents are, the better they are able to accept this. A child brought up with a reasonable degree of independence is able to face this separation well. The child who is brought up overdependently is not able to survive the separation and to commence living his own family life.

It is not at all uncommon to hear couples in difficulty say "He's too close to his mother," or "She calls her mother day and night." In both cases, we probably see evidence of people who are not able to effect the proper degree of separation from their original family. Often this may be couched in terms of the person's claim to have a greater love for his parents or a greater honoring of his parents, but usually it is a coverup for the person's inability to actually move out and develop a family life of his own. In this section of the book, we will follow the child through to adolescence; in the process, we will see some of the problems that develop as he progresses from his earliest years until that time when he is ready to organize his own family life.

Preparation for a good family life requires separation from one's good family. It is also true that the closeness of his family prepares a child for closeness with other adults, which may eventually result in a family life of his own. In other words, it is necessary to be loved in order to learn how to love; it is necessary to live in a good family in order to better produce a good family of one's own.

Herein lie also the seeds for trouble. Should the family life be overly loving, should the life of the child in his family be one characterized by overdependence upon his parents, then he may, because of the quality of his initial family experiences, be unable to develop sufficient detachment from his original family to start his own in an independent way.

One of my psychologist friends put it this way: the tasks of parents toward the children are to "love them, lead them, and let them go." It is the latter that is often most difficult. What happens to the child in his family has far-reaching effects and greatly determines what will happen to his children in his own family.

What makes your child tick?

Just as the world has always been frantically searching for some elixir to prolong life, parents have been desperate for some cardinal rules with which to guide their behavior toward their children, hoping that, because of this knowledge, life would be more pleasant.

I am sorry to report that I do not have the potion; it is a recipe well-guarded by the gods. There is no warranty for twelve months or 12,000 child-miles, whichever comes first. However, there do seem to be some vital concepts about child growth and development that can make bringing up children a more sensible, humane endeavor: seeking, self-selection, and pacing.

1. *Seeking*. One must assume that the human organism known as child is one that is always in active pursuit of life. Any mother of a two- or three-year-old would not doubt this one bit.

That every child, with the exception of those who may be severely retarded, is an active participant in the game of life has some definite implications for parents. For one thing it means that the child is not a sleeper or watcher; he is a doer—and this means that it is part of the parental responsibility to provide the kind of home atmosphere that aids and abets this seeking behavior.

Because TV is such a startling phenomenon for the child does not mean that he must be allowed to lie there hour upon hour in a stupor of gazing. Given an exciting alternative early in life, he will favor the active pursuit of the world around him. Those parents who are content to lie about with their young will not discover that their children are active seekers after the adventure of human existence.

2. *Self-selection.* Children choose and select from all that surrounds them precisely that which they want and need. Indeed, one of the great riddles of rearing and schooling children is that they rarely want or need what we adults feel they should want or need. Yet, you may be certain that theirs is not a passive response to the stimuli around them.

Many years ago a physician discovered that some of his patients who had just given birth were munching away on the walls of the hospital wards. Why? The body has its own wisdom, and it often dictates to us what we should do. After childbirth the body needs calcium to insure the production of milk. Today women munch on calcium lactate pills; years ago the calcium carbonate in the plaster walls was sufficient to satisfy a similar craving.

And so in the matter of feeding children we may be certain that given a wide choice of equally good foods, children will self-select those foods their bodies most need. Thus there is no need to fret about poor eaters. No children set about to starve themselves to death. Given wide choice, they select excellent diets. Of course it isn't nearly as neat as when you feed them, and it isn't nearly as organized as when you dish it up, but eat they will, and all they need, too.

3. *Pacing*. Each child ticks to the pace of his own internal timepiece. He will walk, learn, eat, and sleep when he chooses and for as long as he chooses, as fast as he pleases, and as much as he wants. His pace is individual. Left alone but with proper supervision, he will pace himself in his life, and little may be done to make dire changes in this regard.

Forewarned is forearmed, and what you have just read should help you relax a bit. Your child will find the whole world if you show him some of the way; he will select from it what he really feels he needs, and he will go about all of this in his own fashion, at his particular pace.

And that's what makes him tick, like it or not.

Three types of children today

Just like in the days when cars came in three models, the research of Dr. Stella Chess seems to indicate that almost from the moment of birth there are three readily identifiable types of children. So, sit down for a moment, study these categories, place your children into one of them, and you are well on your way to a better understanding of what makes them either chug along or charge along.

Dr. Chess labels the three types of children as the *easy,* the *difficult,* and the *slow to warm up.* Let's take a look at each type:

1. *The easy child.* These are children who are preponderately positive in mood, highly regular, readily adaptable, low or mild in the intensity of their reactions, and usually affirmative in their approach to new situations. As babies they quickly establish predictable sleeping habits, much to the joy of their parents. They develop regular feeding schedules that coincide with the family's already established pattern. They smile at strangers and easily ingest all kinds of foods. A mother's dream.

As the children grow older, all of these patterns seem to persist. They get on just great in school and adjust to whatever problems confront them. They find the world warm, pleasant, and accepting, and so that is how the world finds them.

That is how it appears at first glance. It is true that they appear to have the least chance of becoming disturbed in later life, and as a group they do have fewer problems. Interestingly, their problems develop *because* of their virtue of adaptability. "Easy" children adapt to their home environment beautifully, but when they move into a world that does not necessarily replicate their home environment—even conflicts with it—they be taken by surprise by the conflict between what they learned at home and their peer, school, or recreational group. Finding themselves the butt of peer scorn because of their inability to shift gears can be upsetting.

2. *Difficult children.* Difficult children are, based upon the description above of easy children, exactly opposite. They are unpredictable, respond to life's stresses with violent tantrums, and make special demands upon everyone around them.

A lengthy study of these children from birth through adolescence revealed that 70 percent of them developed behavior problems. All is not lost, however. Once it is rather clearly ascertained that a child is difficult, the parents need to learn to respond differently than they might with an easy child.

Asking for rapid changes to surrounding conditions is nearly impossible. When parents ask for changes slowly and consistently and with a great deal of patience and understanding, the difficult child can learn the rules for socialization, and he can function effectively.

There is no evidence that the parents cause this child to be difficult; he just came that way. What is a problem is the early and usually consistent angry reaction of the parents to this child. Such hostility toward him simply creates a vicious cycle that frequently results in a very difficult preschooler, an early tumultuous adolescence. To a great extent parental knowledge can effectively diminish this prognosis.

3. *Slow-to-warm-up children.* This child usually has a negative response to many ordinary situations, such as sleeping, feeding, and socializing, but he gradually adapts after repeated contacts with new stimuli. Unlike the difficult child and the easy child, he does not have violent reactions —only mildly negative ones. He does not adapt easily either. Slow adaptation to environmental stimuli is the order of the day.

Vulnerability does not imply inevitability. That is, while it may be perfectly true that the slow-to-warm-up child will finally adapt to life, only more slowly, this we term a vulnerability and nothing more. To make the point more dramatically, the difficult baby does not necessarily turn into an unmanageable monster as he grows up unless his parents do not understand his infant reactions and act accordingly. The usual parental response to the irritable, hot-tempered baby is to be punitive, hateful, and resentful, thus triggering like responses in the child.

In conclusion, one word of caution is in order: Even if you classify your baby as one of these three types, the results are not certain by any means.

The needs of children

Every parent wants to know what a child needs to develop and grow up normally. Sigmund Freud identified a number of psychosexual stages commencing with early infancy. These were the oral, anal, oedipal, latency, and adolescence stages on up to maturity. These formulations, now only partially accepted by even the psychological world, postulate a sexual basis to nearly every phase of development.

Further, Dr. Freud stated that at any time in the development of the child, the child may experience undue difficulty in deriving satisfaction of the needs for that particular period. If this is the case, the developing child will pass on to the next period and leave the demands of the last period unmet. Thus he becomes fixated at a particular level, and his personality is arrested at that point. Only deep analysis will shake the fixation.

Dr. Eric Erikson, a psychologist at Harvard University, has built upon Freud's psychosexual needs and labeled them as "the eight stages of man." In this chapter let us concentrate on the first two stages.

In the first stages of life, from birth to about the first year, the development of a sense of trust is paramount. Dr. Erikson says, "The amount of trust derived from early infantile experience does not seem to depend on absolute quantities of food or demonstrations of love, but rather on the *quality* of their maternal relationships."

While he uses the word *maternal*, it is not necessary that the quality care be given by a child's natural mother. A father or mother substitute is perfectly acceptable provided that figure is sensitive and empathic in response to the infant's discomforts and hungers. Thus a basic pattern of trust in his environment develops, and this may be permanent.

It should be emphasized that a secure infancy is no guarantee of lifetime tranquillity. Early security builds the base or coats the tank against ordinary corrosion, but during any and all of our progression through life, our sense of trust will be tested often.

After the first year of life and until about the third year is the age of autonomy, according to Dr. Erikson. While my behavioral friends may take exception to the entire concept of autonomy, I believe, with Dr. Erikson, that during this period the child is developing control over his bodily processes, while his body is preparing to explore the world around him (he can now walk and talk some), and that he can now develop control that is basically hostile or kindly depending upon his personality and the quality of control exerted by the adults around him.

Since little that is attributable to personality can be conveniently isolated (i.e., while we know that "personality is unique," we are never sure just what personal responses may be directly attributed to one's genes), we need, in a very real and practical sense, to zero in on the significant adults who surround each child. Thus if they exert, in this crucial state, undue restrictions upon the exploratory behavior of the child, he will develop a sense of guilt or shame over his natural urge to explore his life space.

The earliest years and later learning

There is a frantic scurrying these days for *the* answer to why so many children have learning difficulties once they get to school.

Journals report that learning patterns are fixed long before the child enters school. Some specialists think that between the second and third years of life the most crucial events either occur or do not occur, and that these events in and of themselves can accelerate or enhance the learning of children or they can irreversibly retard learning. I suspect that the answer to the question is not possible with the knowledge now at hand.

In the light of much other research on older people, I am not at all convinced that there is a particular year that is *the* critical one. The finding that most impresses me to date indicates that mental abilities increase from infancy to age sixteen, and that after that age there is a distinct leveling off in the electrical responses of the brain. Large brain changes occur during the formative years (birth through six) and reach a peak at five through seven.

Dr. Elie Schneouer has said that his research is absolutely conclusive that nutrition prior to birth is the most significant factor in brain development. His brilliant work builds on the thesis that mental retardation is directly linked to prenatal nutrition intake and utilization during pregnancy. (See *The Malnourished Mind,* New York: Torchbooks, 1974.)

Researchers at the University of Southern California Gerontology Center have shown that older people don't necessarily lose brain cells, and so it is possible to be as bright in our seventies and eighties as we were in our thirties. I cite these examples only because I cannot conceive of anyone daring to try to determine a particular year that a child must be caught and taught in order to guarantee later success in school. Just as there is no particular year at the older end of the spectrum at which one starts to decelerate, so it is illogical to assume that there is one single magic year in childhood.

For many years we thought that if a person missed a particular developmental stage in childhood, irreparable damage would be done to the psyche. In fact, Freud called this an arrestation of development. He and others then went on to say that unless psychotherapy intervened, the person was literally doomed to stay fixed at the limits of his development at the particular time it was arrested.

Modern child-development theory admits that there are stages; for example, the first year of life is considered to be very important for developing a sense of trust versus mistrust between an infant and the rest of the world. But as important as this is, should a child have a very rocky start, all is not lost. The sense of trust is something we are continually developing throughout our lives, and it may become a crisis at any time. If, however, we have been brought up with a solid sense of trust for the world around us, the next disappointment we have will not be as traumatic.

An extreme statement by Dr. Burton White, director of the preschool project at Harvard University, notes that "if a child is six months or more behind in academically relevant areas, such as language and problem-solving skills, at age three, he is not likely ever to be successful in his future educational career."

Despite such findings or hypotheses, I myself cannot find any hard evidence that selecting the age of three is any more scientific than, say, four or five. Dr. Jerome Kagan, also of Harvard, reports that children in South America who are literally raised in airless, dark rooms and given no parental attention for the first years of their lives, are by eleven in no way different from North American children given the usual affection, play space, etc., that is their lot.

In their text *Child Development: A Core Approach* (Wiley, 1972), Weiner and Elkind say this about children in some American Indian tribes who are strapped to a cradle board for almost all of their waking hours: "They still stand, walk and crawl at the same ages as do children who have not been so restrained. Environmental circumstances must be very extreme before they begin to alter in any lasting way a child's inherent pace of growth in height, weight and motor skills."

None of the foregoing is cited to suggest that there aren't many activities that, when wisely used during the preschool years, cannot be fun, advantageous, and even instructive. It is to say that people are too panicked by the thought that they have somehow missed a rare opportunity when the third or fifth birthday has passed.

Helping your child before school starts

If you are the typical mother with a preschool-age child or two at home, then you are probably very concerned about making certain that child will be academically successful in school. I think I can help you.

As far as I know, there isn't any magic food or vitamin that will do it. When I was a child my mother insisted that fish was brain food. My, how we laughed at her silly old wives tale! Since then, I have come to understand that we are what we eat, both physically and intellectually. Consider that every shred of evidence indicates that protein intake during fetal development is crucial. Thus, when Mom called fish brain food, she was in her unscientific way absolutely correct.

I have it on good authority that the development of the brain has two critical periods. The first is in the fifteenth week of development through the twentieth week. The second great spurt takes place from the twenty-fifth week until the age of two. This means that fetal malnutrition may be especially critical at these times.

To insure your child's success in school, it is important

that not only prior to and during pregnancy, but also during the first two years of life, care is taken as to the quality of food ingested, making certain that there is plenty of protein and little cola and fried potatoes in his diet.

Next, remember that the quality of the relationship between husband and wife is very important so that the child goes to school with as little anxiety as possible. The roots of some school failure do lie in the home.

Assuming a healthy emotional climate at home and proper nutrition from conception until at least the second year of life, what else needs to be done to assure school success?

Dr. Burton White of the Harvard Graduate School of Education concluded, after studying the parents of academically successful children, that such parents tend to talk a great deal to their children, provide many interesting things to see and touch, have plenty of energy and patience, and are not too concerned about their children's breaking things and messing up the house.

Dr. Gabriel Della-Piana, in his book *How to Talk with Children (and other People)* (New York: John Wiley and Sons, 1973), reports on results of using some highly effective self-teaching and self-correcting programmed-learning techniques and gives a large number of very specific parental behaviors likely to elicit the kinds of verbal responses from children than will help in their intellectual growth. He does not, however, say that these ways of responding to children will increase intellect. He suggests that we may scold, accept, question, explain, direct, distract, and ignore children by our answers to their concerns. When children live in an atmosphere of general acceptance and support, the family environment is more conducive to developing a more fully functioning child, thus creating a better learner.

Another timely book is Dr. T. H. Bell's *Your Child's Intellect* (Salt Lake City: Olympus Publishing Company, 1972). In it, Dr. Bell, who is now United States Commissioner of Education, speaks of home-based education and provides a veritable gold mine of suggestions for parents who wish to prepare their children for optimum success in school. One word of caution, however: Helping to create the conditions to ensure school success can be messy and noisy. If either of these things annoy you, then Dr. Bell's suggestions will hurt.

If you do all of the things these and other authors talk about, will you guarantee success in school? Barring a host of such unforeseen circumstances as emotional problems, schools and teachers that somehow frighten the child, and the influence of genetics, I think there is a strong assurance that your child will not be hurt by what you will gain from them. Common sense is uncommon enough. With this sense and some direction, you can at least be sure your child will not spend his preschool days sitting before the TV set and doing nothing else. But if you just buy or borrow these volumes, there is no warranty, unless you take the theories and try them. Both enriching environments and changing behavior take persistent efforts.

Competition— does it help or hinder the child?

"Competition to Americans is like apple pie." "Competition has made us what we are today." "Competition kills the spirit." "Competition engenders hate." Each of these statements has some truth in it—yet the real truth about competition lies somewhere in between. But where?

Permit me to make some statements that I know to be true about human growth and development, and then let's see where we are with the whole competition issue. The word *some* is probably the real key here. *Some* children thrive on the challenge offered by competition.

In my book *You and Your Child's World* (Deseret Book, 1967), I reported on the very bad sibling relations that developed between two brothers because their mother continually compared them. In fact, so bitter was their childhood relationship that those bad feelings persist today.

On the other hand, I know a sister team where the older thrived upon the keen competition engendered by the family. Indeed, one might fairly say that she "became" because of the competition between the two.

If I were forced to commit myself to an actual percentage split between the innate love of competition and the deleterious effects of it, I would say that 40 percent of all children will thrive on reasonable competitive incentives, and 60 percent will be hurt by it. When intense competition is involved, I would say that 20 percent would not be adversely affected, and 80 percent would be considerably disturbed.

In and of itself, competition isn't all bad. An individual child's response to competition should be the ultimate criterion by which parents decide whether or not to foster it.

For children who seem to thrive upon pitting themselves against others, I would say that a reasonably competitive atmosphere could be highly motivating and advantageous. In other words, a child's response to the competitive environment should be carefully studied, and then a decision regarding the use of competition can be more intelligently made.

Let me give an example from my own family's experience. I have a fourteen-year-old son who has taken tennis instruction from some great professionals. At twelve he really caught on and was playing beautifully. Since we belong to a tennis club, the competitive tennis environment is very much around us.

At any time of the day and night one can see earnest parents who never made the grade in tennis stardom, as well as parents whose names are legendary in tennis, grooming their children for highly competitive tennis. *Grooming* is perhaps too kind a word. In some cases *grueling* their children is more applicable!

Now, for some children this is fine. They flourish under

the regime. However, I watched my son in one tournament and could see the obvious distaste with which he approached the prospect of defeat. He won, and I shall never forget the bitter tears of his opponent. When I spoke with my son about the experience, when I placed that information into a father's computer, which had for twelve years been registering the emotions of a boy, I realized that this child was not built for intense competition, and since then I have never stressed competitiveness.

There is much talk about the fully functioning person being an "inner-directed" individual. More simply put, this means that the best-adjusted human beings don't need to have others prodding them to excel. The truth about the matter is that only the unusual child scours the home when asked to clean. Only the rare student delves so deeply into materials that the teacher is astounded by his assiduousness.

The task of rearing humans who don't need to be threatened or prodded is monumental, and I cannot prescribe the solution. A human being turned on by any cause is a remarkable creature. Once he is internally motivated, the amount of progress that he will make without competing with anyone else is phenomenal.

Some children, as well as adults, are not internally motivated. They need something other than their own drive to propel them. Some types of competition may be excellent, while other forms may produce anxiety beyond measure, even trauma.

In Japan it is not unusual to have many suicides after the announcements have been made about those eligible for the four-year universities. The competition is so severe that it traumatizes some persons.

Regardless of the type of child you have, here are some general rules to help your family live best with mild competition:

First, try to stress the joy of accomplishment rather than the victory. Help your children to savor self-satisfaction. It is the most powerful character builder known.

Next, never make your love and approval totally dependent upon victories over others. High-level achievement in any area of endeavor must not be equated with personal worth.

Finally, if competition is the order of the day for your child, be as certain as possible that it is therapeutic competition wherein the victory over other human beings does not become the be-all and end-all of life.

Money and character development

Over 200 years ago Thomas Jefferson said this about the American dilemma: "Yes, we did produce a near perfect Republic. But will they keep it, or will they, in the enjoyment of plenty, lose the memories of freedom? Material abundance without character is the surest way to destruction."

While it is no fun to be poor, it is equally hazardous to be rich. One of the shames of our affluent times is that money has turned the hearts of many from their families. I should correct that statement. Money in and of itself can do nothing. It is the love of it that can destroy. Character is never easy to acquire. Having too much money makes it even more difficult.

Too many perfectly lovely people, especially young mothers, have told me that things were okay at their homes until their husbands started to make money.

It takes an extremely well-disciplined person not to start having dreams of glory when his dreams of money have come true. Few children can survive the curse of parents who give them everything, whether they need it or not.

Children are unable to resist the indolent, arrogant attitude that creeps upon them when they lack nothing.

Isn't it strange that the abundance of money has always been the subject of man's musings? Matthew tells us that "it is easier for a camel to pass through the eye of a needle, than for a rich man to enter into the kingdom of God." (Matthew 19:24.)

Indeed, the cynicism about money and wealth has plagued Eastern European Jewry until this very day. One proverb says, "If the rich could hire others to die for them, the poor could make a nice living."

Children must not be bought. I know a couple who make the payoff every report-card time. An A equals one dollar. Too often these same people resort to the trickery of money to persuade their children to be righteous.

I can never forget the gentleman who came to me with the tale of how he, in order to teach his children how much $5,000 was, arranged for a dinner in a local restaurant and placed 5,000 one-dollar bills in a pile before his family. At the proper moment in the evening he dramatically swept the cover from the mound of bills, exposing the treasure, and then told his family that for each of them there was this initial payment if they would only promise to tread the straight and narrow.

The finest thing a civilized person can do with his money is to perhaps gather his children around and discuss with them ways of disbursing it to those who have not. Most of us have not always had it too easy, and so if we happen to strike it rich, whether accidentally or from hard labor, we need to remember that our children are not made better and their character is not increased by a surfeit of riches.

I must hasten to say that extreme penuriousness isn't a good example either. Children must learn what it means to work, what it means not to have, what saving and even scrounging really means.

Too many of us are emotional prisoners of our past, and we want to make it easier for our loved ones. In an effort to remind the people how little money really meant, Eastern Jewry had this saying: "Shrouds are made without pockets." President David O. McKay wisely counseled that "no other success can compensate for failure in the home."

Fat paychecks, property, snowmobiles, huge automobiles and boats, and other outward signs of success and material abundance can never substitute for a parent who cares enough to teach his family to earn a reasonable share of their plush existence.

Have youngsters changed?

People over forty are fond of clucking to themselves about the fact that "things—and especially children—ain't what they used to be." I myself used to be one who chided my generation by saying that they had simply forgotten what things were like, and in retrospect, days gone by took on a haze or glaze. Time had dulled recollection even as Jacob of old was deceived, because of his age, into administering a blessing to the wrong son.

I am now convinced that I was wrong and that many children today are, in fact, infantalized. That is, they exhibit brief attention spans, they are unable to work toward goals, they expect instant gratification for whatever they do, and they are passive waiters rather than doers.

This curious inability to delay gratification, the unusual involvement only with the present, their need to conform, and their insatiable thirst to consume have made them different from those of us born in the 1920s. What kind of parents they will make is a tantalizing question whose answer is already beginning to take shape.

I recollect Dr. Howard Lane, my chief graduate adviser

and one-time psychologist to the Detroit Police Department, saying that even in the 1950s children weren't what they used to be. As he put it, "I was born and reared in LeRoy, Kansas, on a farm. There was work to do and I was there to do it. I was needed, significant, and the mainstay of a family."

You might ask yourself if any one of your children really feels needed. Is it possible—in today's disposable diaper, hypodermic needle, and disposable spouse age—for any child to feel as if his contributions were really vital to the ongoingness of his family?

About the only work I can contrive for my son is the Monday night ritual of taking out the garbage, and should that be too arduous, we can always borrow my neighbor's aluminum garbage cart to pull the cans to the curb only thirty-eight feet away. Other than that, he isn't at all necessary to the economic or social survival of the family. He knows this, and so do I. Thus it was with total joy that I recently observed a slight preference he showed for our new-old hand mower over the gas-eating, smoke-belching rotary we had just bought.

Now I don't think there is a way back to my days in which, incidentally, I was of not much more use, since we never even took out our own garbage. In my New York City apartment the dumbwaiter bell would ring each night at five, and we'd go to that dumbwaiter door in the kitchen, open it, and deposit our refuse for the day on the little wooden platform before us. Then we'd call out "O.K.," and our building superintendent, known by the not-so-baffling title of "super," would pull the ropes of the dumbwaiter and away would go the garbage.

Rural life seems to be about over, as far as its being a real part of most Americans' lives is concerned. Even on my Uncle Bill's chicken farm, where once each year for a brief week or so I'd make vain attempts to carry a sack of feed to the feed barrel, things aren't the same. Bill has everything automatic now. The only thing he never has been able to control is the awful truth that on the day he agreed to sell his chickens, the market dropped four cents, which was his anticipated profit. I think I really have a feeling for the song about "owing one's soul to the company store"!

No small blame for the infantalization of our youth may be placed at the door of the industrialization of America. Though 85 percent of our automobiles are never fully owned, they are discarded every three years. Pills give people instant relief; drugs, rapid withdrawal from whatever is unbearable in the world.

Everything the country dreams of comes prepackaged, precooked, immediately available. From credit to cornices, nothing takes much time. Students thrive on minicourses that gloss over hard study; we even test our youth with rapid personality assessments. Millions of children watch adult and juvenile drama on TV where no more than two to three minutes pass without a quick change of scene, mood, and character.

The playing fields look busy, but countless millions have learned to watch sports and not actively participate. Wars without end have convinced folks that life's goals are but fantasies, since "tomorrow we die." For the first time in man's history two nations have enough destructive capacity (overkill) to completely destroy every inhabitant of each country more than 300 times—as if once weren't enough!

You wanted answers, didn't you. Well, we can't abdicate now, nor stop the world or say we want to get off. No one wants to turn back. We have sown seeds; now we reap the grim harvest. Only the home and family can create its limited microcosms and develop its own values.

Even here the world can't be shut out entirely. It is urgent that each family be in the world, yet be idiosyncratic enough to develop its own life-style, where its unique values will prevail, without ill-equipping the children to live successfully in the asphalt jungle.

The adolescent hassle

A tearful mother called me the other night threatening to send her teenage daughter out of the house forever unless something happened to alter her adolescent behavior. "She screams, she torments, she demands, she rants and raves, she tells me I'm stupid, and I can't stand her," lamented the mother.

Now the phone is no place to try to solve the adolescent hassle, and so there really was little anyone could do just then. Let's see what makes the adolescent tick or rattle or call it what you will. Adolescence is a hassle and always has been.

Whatever you may or may not think about Anna Freud, she did understand adolescence. If none of what I quote in the next few lines resembles your adolescent, I would be surprised. In her volume *The Psychoanalytic Study of the Child,* she says:

"It is normal for an adolescent to behave in an inconsistent and unpredictable manner; to fight his impulses and accept them; to love his parents and to hate them; to be deeply ashamed to acknowledge his mother before others, and unexpectedly desire heart-to-heart talks with her; to thrive on imitation and identify with others, while searching unceasingly for his own identity; to be more idealistic, artistic, generous, and unselfish than he ever will be again, but also the opposite: self-centered, egoistic, calculating.

"Such fluctuations between extreme opposites would be deemed highly abnormal at any other time of life. At this time, they may signify no more than that an adult structure of personality takes a long time to emerge, that the ego of the individual in question does not cease to experiment, and is in no hurry to close down on possibilities."

So now you know what Anna Freud says. But what does it all mean for you, living in your family with your teenagers today?

Let's take some of the characteristics noted above and discuss their implications for parental behavior.

Too often we expect our adolescents to follow through perfectly on their goals and promises. There are times when they do. Quite often they do, and then with a startling turnabout, they don't. Remember, Anna Freud said that they were "inconsistent and unpredictable." This in no way means that you accept all such behavior. It does mean that sometimes it is really sort of fun to observe them and their inconsistencies and enjoy this growth period.

The two most difficult things for a parent to accept about youthful behavior are the frequent challenging of our closely held ideas and having our children ridicule us either privately or publicly.

Under usual circumstances you may be assured that your children love you. That they cannot show it or demonstrate it, or even may deny it, does not negate this truth. In their striving for identity and independence, it sometimes becomes necessary to hate the ones you love.

The verbal brashness and insolence are part of that struggle to break away, and teenagers do not know how to accomplish it without devastating their parents. Countless mothers have wrung their hands and wondered what they could have done to spark such antagonism. This is another time when a little knowledge allows the wise parent to tolerate certain verbal and nonverbal indiscretions. You see, whenever tomorrow may come, that child will almost suddenly turn around and seek comfort and advice. This door between you needs to be kept open and swinging.

What too frequently happens is that in their demands for respect and cordiality, parents turn off these children, so that nasty language becomes a way of life and, in fact, all lines of communication break.

Parents who expect aberrations from their children are better able to absorb a reasonable degree of negative feelings because they see them as a sure sign of the developing adult. Once the battle lines have been drawn and there is no exchange other than from the insolent teenager to his parents, all that I have said will seem Utopian and optimistic.

We suggested earlier that the adolescent thrives on imitation, yet is really striving for his own identity. One parent asked me why his son doesn't try imitating him instead of his "no good" friends. Good question. He doesn't emulate his parents because he has a more imperious call from his peers, who for quite a while will be his dictators. The tyranny of the peer group during adolescence is often a fearsome thing and a factor not easily overcome by anxious parents. The teenager must imitate his own because they govern his world in a way that parents can't.

And yet, through all this browbeating that he takes at their hands, he is surely and slowly creating an inner mechanism, a style he will one day not be afraid to exhibit, but which for the present must not surface, lest the peer group blow it out of the sea of adolescence. Incidentally, whatever surfaces will more likely resemble your life-style than anyone else's.

Let me conclude with this supportive statement by the most respected specialist in human growth and development living today, Erik H. Erikson. In his famous work *Childhood and Society*, he says this about the adolescent:

"The growing and developing youths, faced with... tangible adult tasks ahead of them, are now primarily concerned with what they appear to be in the eyes of others as compared with what they feel they are....

"In their search for a new sense of continuity and sameness, adolescents have to refight many of the battles of earlier years, even though to do so they must artificially appoint perfectly well-meaning people to play the role of adversaries; and they are ever ready to install lasting idols and ideas as guardians of a final identity."

The teenager's parents and his family are his adversaries, his peers become his idols, and some pretty weird activities and occupations become his ideal. With a little bit of luck he will return to the ideals of his family, but not without struggle and heartache for all concerned.

Young adulthood

In the adolescent years there is the continual struggle for what Harvard psychologist Dr. Erik Erikson calls identity. During this time one's sexual identity and social values—ideology, so to speak—begin to coalesce. During this time there is much testing again of beginning human relationships, which will one day become what Dr. Erikson terms a "sense of intimacy."

When a young person has passed through the last stages of adolescence, at about the ages of twenty-one to twenty-five, and has successfully developed a sense of self, an identity, then he is ready to affiliate more closely with another of the opposite sex.

During all of the preceding years of development, there has been a steadily developing confidence (or lack of it) in the self. There has been a continuity of development. This is not to say that there haven't been crises. The crises have been reasonably met, however, and the individual is ready to move on in his progress to maturity. In other words, he has integrated his childhood experiences sufficiently so that he has power and confidence in himself.

Now comes the time between about twenty-five and the early forties when the strengths acquired up to this time need to transcend themselves and focus on marriage. Whereas before there was much self-gratification, much ego-centeredness, there now comes the time when there is a desire to fuse one's identity with that of another. Dr. Erikson puts it this way: "He is ready for intimacy; that is, the capacity to commit himself to concrete affiliations and partnerships and to develop the ethical strength to abide by such commitments, even though they may call for significant sacrifices and compromises." *(Childhood and Society,* New York: W. W. Norton, 1950, p. 263.)

The mark of the adult is the *ethical* sense—that is, the commitment to intimacy, which is more than fleeting. It seems rather clear to me that one of the reasons for failure in marriage, particularly teenage marriage, is that the resolution of the identity crisis is not usually achieved by either of the two children who get married. Thus there is no real readiness for a commitment to an ethical, binding relationship one with another. It is extremely difficult for either one to feel irrevocably bound to himself first.

As one reads about communal marriage, he is struck by the impermanence of both the community and the people within the commune. This phenomenon is particularly true with respect to the male's communal commitment, which is too frequently tenuous. This has been referred to as the "splitting phenomenon," meaning that these fathers feel free to split or leave whenever they are so moved.

I submit that where the ego-identity crisis has been reasonably resolved and has thus prepared one to enter into an ethical relationship with a member of the opposite sex, the "splitting phenomenon" is reduced to a minimum. Thus, by inference, I am also willing to say that those who live communal lives still long for the benign paternalism of their original family. They are not psychosocially prepared to enter into durable relationships, so they escape into communities that cater to their infantile wishes to be footloose and fancyfree and to split when they please; and when they do split, they leave mother and child behind to fend for themselves and to take up with whomever they can.

One cannot love another ethically until he is ready to commit himself irrevocably to that other person. Old hat? Perhaps so, but there are too many young women in America who bought the "do your own thing," lawless philosophy and who today stand forlorn and bedraggled, wondering how they ever let themselves be so used. Neither they nor their mates were really ready for any more than the biology of life. They threw themselves into this situation with little thought for a coalition intended to produce a responsible generation.

Sex education for boys

A father who thinks he can start a friendship with his son when the boy is eleven is, of course, seriously mistaken. The traditional "birds and bees" discussion just doesn't "take" when it is in the form of the first deep communication between the two.

What does a boy need to know? All that he needs to know about sex has been the subject of dozens of books. Allow me to focus for a bit upon the earliest pubertal years —around age eleven or so.

Assuming reasonable physical development, we can assume that increasingly the boy will become very much more aware of his mother as a member of the opposite sex. Fathers and mothers need to realize that this awareness is sexual. There is no other word for it; no euphemism will replace this bold fact. And when, for the second time in his life, a boy becomes sexually aware of his mother (the first time was when he was a preschooler), it is very likely that he will feel guilty about associating her with erotic fantasies.

In my opinion, folks who refuse to recognize the truth of this have successfully forgotten their own childhoods.

The boy will bury his guilt and anxiety because it is very disturbing, and this is where a father can help.

A father needs to be in close-enough contact with his son so that he can verbalize these feelings. You see, his son cannot easily live with his mother when he views her as a sex object. So strong is the guilt over this that mothers often complain that their twelve-, thirteen-, and fourteen-year-old sons seem to hate them. One mother told me that she felt as if she had suddenly become her son's enemy. He verbally assaulted her, physically avoided her, and was so generally obnoxious that the poor young woman wondered if the evil gods had taken possession of what a few years earlier was a genteel human being who couldn't be torn from her side the day kindergarten started!

A father's role here, then, is to be able to tell his son that he once felt the same way. One caution, however: Overzealous dads too often tell too much, too soon, and a nine- or ten-year-old or younger boy really can't manage this totally baffling information. A boy should hear this from his dad when mom reports she feels the beginning of hate and rejection. And while it is urgent that mothers understand what father and son are discussing, mother is not the proper person to be providing a boy's sex education after he's nine or ten.

Fathers who cannot or will not become this primary source of a boy's understanding of himself need to be sure that some other male figure will. This is easy to say, I know, but difficult to provide. However, teachers, Scout or religious leaders are often excellent resources. We don't need a unit of planned intellectual content either. What is needed is the right moment and developmental level, the breath of confidence that must exist between two or more humans.

The failure of mass sex education programs is that they are spewed forth from strangers who happen to teach civics or health. Sex education ought to be a personal, dynamic interaction between folks who are genuinely concerned with each other's welfare. That's why fathers and sons, rather than programmed courses, are natural conduits.

On more than one occasion professionals in child development have heard of boys who even at seventeen and eighteen have had no normal boy-girl friendships. The inability to relate to females as human beings generally springs from unresolved emotional conflicts that arose during early puberty.

A boy's thoughts of his mother as a sexual object are shocking to him. Most religiously oriented boys are, in fact, likely to be profoundly shocked about their corporeal feelings for their mothers. Unless the boy is helped to realize that this is part of normal male development and that with time it will pass, these thoughts can be disturbing enough to arrest normal heterosexual development and to force him to take cover from his guilty feelings by stopping further association with all women.

Thus, a father should be the primary source of a boy's sexual knowledge. He can be very instrumental in relieving the anxiety of his son's sexual feelings for not only his mother but also for other females in the house. A young boy can become obsessed with feelings of depravity for having these impulses toward the people with whom he has grown up. If one of those persons, his father, can relieve him of this feeling, a giant step forward in his emotional development will have been achieved.

The stereotype of dad as merely a breadwinner should long ago have been relegated to the scrap heap of family folkways.

Counseling adolescent virginity

Whether or not to engage in sexual relations before marriage has been a problem disturbing to adolescents since time began. For whatever reason, man was created so that at the height of his sexual prowess he is usually unmarried. In other words, during the high school and college years, human beings are most interested and able to engage in sexual behavior, which has been declared impossible or immoral except within the marriage contract.

A cruel trick of fate? This is hard to say.

Again, apart from theological admonitions, especially from the more orthodox and conservative religious movements, there has been, in this country at least, a large segment of society that has dismissed ancient admonitions and urged "living it up" in every way.

When I was preparing for marriage back in the 1950s in New York City, one of the expected gifts was some sort of marriage manual that would introduce the couple into secrets never shared by parents and their children. Indeed, such a book was considered indispensable to any couple ready to marry, since it was assumed that each had had no prior experience.

In 1973 there is probably little need for such instruction, since any movie rated PG or R is far more explicit than the tender words of Dr. Van der Velde's text. Anything rated X, of course, presumes a great deal of experience.

Recently, Dr. Richard V. Lee, director of the medical clinics of Yale University School of Medicine, wrote an interesting article for the New York *Times* ("What About the Right to Say 'No?'," September 16, 1973) in which he defends chastity publicly, which is, to say the least, a brave thing to do in the traditionally liberal Eastern Establishment. Some of what he says I find unusually candid and correct.

One of the awkward things for parents today is to attempt to discuss sexual matters with their children. Most parents of teenagers simply assume that it is taken for granted that today's liberated adolescents know all there is to know. Not so, says Dr. Lee, who contends that adolescents are as ambivalent and anxious about sex as were their parents. He says that while there has been a youth rebellion against Victorian morality, instead of liberating youth it has transformed sex into an ideology.

This new ideology says that sex is good and that anybody can and ought to indulge. He observes that the pleasures of sex have been transformed into duty. Most "with it" kids feel that if for some reason they haven't experienced sex before they are fifteen, they will go crazy. The current word in that group is that chastity is a *hang-up*.

While Dr. Lee isn't wild about the prudery of Victorian purity, he finds the new sexual ideology as dictatorial and cruel as that of prudery.

Virginity is an acceptable way of life. There is nothing crazy about anyone who believes that, until the right time comes, that is the way he should live. Considering chastity harmful—as the superliberal do—is a sign of sick adolescent minds, no matter how old the folks who espouse such a philosophy.

It is true that all young people have sexual impulses; in many they are very strong. This is not a sign of moral decay. Too many, I fear, wish youth to deny even having the impulses. Not to want to do anything about those impulses is a matter of personal concern and commitment. It does not indicate that persons so acting are immature, sick, square, or dogmatic.

One of our troubles today is that the older generation has accepted the vision of the promiscuous adolescent, and they have been so intimidated by it that they dare not raise their voices against what has been ordained by the high priests of the drug cult.

Once adults understand the myths of adolescent sexual behavior, they will recognize that most young people, given some adult support, would like to live lives uncomplicated by a type of sexual behavior that gets in the way of establishing deep and intimate human relationships.

Sexual relations are important in deepening the relationships between adults. When they are confined to behavior between married people, they stimulate deepening feelings.

When it characterizes the goal of the relationships between adolescents, the desire for sexual gratification is stronger than the desire to develop any other part of the relationship. Thinking that sex isn't a commitment that can hurt when that relationship is broken is bad thinking. When a sexual relationship ends, there is isolation and rejection. If young people really are serious about developing honest human relationships, then they must face up to the fact that sex on a trial basis is as cruel and as "using" as is marriage on such a basis.

My plea to all adults is not to overestimate your children and not to underestimate yourselves. At no time in history has youth been the repository of all wisdom. The experiences and problems you went through as an adolescent are the same experiences and problems your children are having. Though they may be more ecologically or even sociologically aware, they are repeating your own youthful dilemmas. Their hair is longer, their jeans more raggedy, but deep within their hearts they yearn for parental guidance and discipline as they face their sexuality in a world reeling from promiscuity and amoral attitudes. If you don't give them some assurances of a value system that is decent, they will not find it in their peer group.

Chastity is not sick. Our so-called sexual liberation is another form of enslavement. Parents who behave without sexual promiscuity in *their* lives will give strength to the many youths who yearn for an example. Society is experiencing sexual tyranny, not sexual freedom, when young people are ridiculed for saying no to sexual adventures.

Lost love

Sooner or later if you have a teenager around the house, there will come a day when he will think his world has ended—because of a broken romance. No amount of parental experience and advice will really make much of a difference when this disaster hits. So, what is a parent to do?

Love that is lost is like money in the bank. Left alone for a bit, it increases in value. So, too, the anguish of the adolescent is more likely to help his ultimate growth than to seriously stunt it. But you can't tell the teenager that. There is always a certain amount of suffering that each of us must do by ourselves without the tears of others mingling with our own.

The best thing for a parent to do is to accept the misery, reflect its depth (even shallowness), and assure the hurt child that home is a haven for him where he's wanted and loved.

Too often, when we finally hear the tale of woe, we assume that it is the parents' function to help make the experiences pass away. When we believe thus, we say things like this: "Don't be silly, it's probably better this way." Or, "It is all for the best." Or, "So what? Everyone has to go through it. I did, and so did your dad."

What we have really communicated, however, is a denial of the child's hurt. A parent who denies the depth of such a hurt telegraphs a message of nonconcern—but you *are* concerned, even as hurt and miserable as your child.

Imagine this scene: Your nineteen-year-old daughter has come home from a date with a boy she has been dating for some months, perhaps for as long as a year. She runs into your room, throws herself across the bed, and sobs uncontrollably.

Daughter: It's all over.
Mother (or father): What happened?
Daughter: We talked quite a while tonight and it seemed clear that we had really never understood where each stood on some pretty important issues.
Mother: Do you want to talk about it now?
Daughter: Okay, but it's all over, and I will never see him again.
Mother: Sounds serious. Tell me about it.
Daughter: It *is* serious. I'm really very upset. I think I shall never like anyone again. I couldn't—not after this terrible experience.
Mother: Mmmm. Well, let's hear the whole story.

There were, as you may have noted, a number of places for mother to have responded with such phrases as, "That's silly, it's not over," or, "You'll see, he'll call you tomorrow. It will all blow over." Instead, in my vignette, the mother said little except to agree with what she heard.

The daughter's appraisal of her past love life may be very accurate for her. In fact, it is exactly how it seems to her. To do other than encourage her to tell the whole story would be to transmit the message that you reject her assessment of the situation. True, you may actually reject it, but keep it to yourself, and get your teenager to express her feelings. Often, once she does, the magnitude of the event seems not as momentous.

Heartbreak at eighteen is very important. It is an experience that makes for the savoring of another love a bit later on. We may love many in our lives—and it is right that we should. Nevertheless, the adolescent who has just been hurt is not ready for a complete understanding of this beautiful phenomenon. His or her emotions are very much focused on the love of today and yesterday and not on the statistical probabilities of tomorrow's loves.

Advice rarely suffices. However, you can try detailing the good alternatives that are possible under the circumstances and let the adolescent select the one his head and heart dictate. More importantly, allow him every opportunity to talk, even endlessly, about it. Then his own intelligence will point the healing way.

Middle class rip-off

Four youths pulled into a gas station not too long ago. One was of legal age; the others were below driving age. It was a self-service place, and they filled up their aging Oldsmobile with five dollars worth of gas. Then one of the younger ones was asked to go into the station's office and pay the bill. He had a ten-dollar bill in his hand. The attendant, a young boy, apparently read the figures on the wrong pump, and he gave the teenager seven dollars in change.

Once in the car the boy, laughing, turned the change over to his older sibling. As they drove off, the laughter was louder. They had really pulled a fast one on that dumb kid who couldn't read the right pump.

In the adult world this is called white-collar crime. It isn't approaching the brashness of the kid who packs a Saturday Night Special and makes the rounds of the town's gas stations heisting each one for a couple of bucks. It isn't like the sick kid who lifts social security checks on the first of the month and forges signatures.

This experience didn't start out with any evil intent or

necessity. It was a simple mistake on the part of an attendant who couldn't be sure which pump was used and so he chose the wrong one. Everyone in the car knew which pump had been used. The driver knew how much the bill was. The boy who carried in the ten-dollar bill didn't lie—the attendant just hadn't asked how much the bill was.

In the adult world this kind of crime is glossed over because no one intended to cheat anyone.

When the incident was reported at home, the father of these children was furious. He lectured, cajoled, and asked where he had set so bad an example. One of the children invoked the ancient *caveat emptor*—"let the buyer beware." The parents were incredulous. Could this be their children? Where were the cherished values they were so patiently trying to instill? From what do children really learn. Whom were they modeling themselves after? Where was their example?

The lessons learned in a family are cumulative, adding up to a basic sort of commitment that becomes full-blown or mature when the person himself is mature. Too many parents flagellate themselves when their six-year-old, whom they had so carefully taught, lies; and when he does, they see themselves as the villains. A six-year-old needing to twist the world into the shape he wants will lie in order to make that shape become real.

And so on into adolescence. I can't think of any behavior commonly indulged in by adolescents that their parents haven't railed about for umpteen years—the need for associating with the "right" kinds of friends, trustworthiness, dressing appropriately for the occasion, selecting a "good" girl, living up to promises, etc. It's just that the adult moralities have not been learned by the children; that is, under specific circumstances, all of the lectures, modeling, Sunday School lessons, family and cultural influences haven't had a *profound* impact.

This is not to say that the code you have promulgated all along hasn't had an influence. It has. It is just that at a specific moment when a certain desired goal is particularly appetizing to the maturing mind and body, even the most pervasive of doctrines can go unheeded. The despicable statement that "every man has his price" has too often been proved correct of late, though it seems entirely appropriate as we look at children's behavior.

In other words, the most closely held standards can be compromised when the proper stimulation to bend is exerted. Among those who would not be malleable in the face of any persuasion have come the world's martyrs. Children aren't martyrs. They are in the process of becoming adults. Remember the little girl who when asked "Who made you?" answered, "I don't know, I ain't done yet." Children erring on occasion need to be understood. This does not mean, however, that adults should ever uphold bad behavior when the code has clearly been broken.

Whether six or sixty, we are all responsible for behavior appropriate to our age. We pay a price for treading the primrose path of dalliance. That price hurts us and those children who commit the crime. It is a good hurt.

You will be happy to know that all four culprits mentioned above returned the "stolen" money and admitted their theft to the gas station owner.

Two of those four kids were mine.

Religion and revolt

"In the last three months my son has done a complete flip-flop. For seventeen years he was everything we dreamed a boy should be, but in the last three months he has rejected everything we've ever taught him—especially our religion."

So spoke a distraught father as he and his wife tried to fathom the religious revolt of their adolescent.

Such a revolt may occur as a child moves from childhood into adolescence, because at this time there is a continual exploration of self and the values of one's family and society. There are three major areas the adolescent explores—religion, social idealism, and sex.

By definition adolescence is a movement toward independence, a searching for one's own set of values and standards. Of course, no religion or philosophy anyone subscribes to is his own. That is, few of us develop our own religions. For the most part we either accept or reject what some others have accepted or rejected.

Since adolescence is a sometimes frantic search for identity (selfhood), it is inevitable that the child will examine carefully that which, up to this time, he has had little opportunity to accept or reject for himself. Thus, the process of self-examination often results in change in religious ideals, either in abandonment or increased fervor.

According to a book by the Group for the Advancement of Psychiatry, *The Joys and Sorrows of Parenthood* (New York: Charles Scribner's Sons, 1973), "In order to carry out this process of testing and questioning, adolescents need to be exposed to some structure or order of religion or humanistic values."

Thus, the despair of the parent mentioned above may now be seen in this context: not so much the child rejecting his father's religion out of hand and doing so suddenly, but rather as a natural adolescent response to the value system he had no hand in shaping. That this family imposed a specific religious code upon their son is a tribute to their wisdom. Again, the book just cited says, "It may well be that permissiveness and obscurity in religion give the adolescent nothing to rebel against or depend on."

The normal adolescent needs to have something to battle that is, in a very real sense, equal to and directly associated with his parents, especially his father. Thus, the move toward independence that must gradually be achieved if a healthy adult is to ensue requires equating parents (often dad for the boy and mom for the girl) with religion. If the adolescent rejects their religion (usually temporarily), he is, in reality, rejecting his parents but is passing it off as religious rejection, which is less personal and less emotional. In the process, parents who do not fully comprehend this may feel that they have failed, begin to hate themselves, and seek to blame one another.

The religious revolt of adolescents is understandable, even normal. It becomes irrevocable when the parents overreact and thus make their children's return to them and religion a matter of pride.

An open letter to junior high school teachers

Dear Martyrs: It has long been my belief that you only have one nervous system to give for the school board. Once that is gone, there are no retreads. A nervous system that is "shot" takes years to mend. We have given you our twelve-, thirteen-, and fourteen-year-old children. Professor Howard Lane used to say that a certain number of fleas is good for a dog because it takes his mind off being a dog. It seems to me that a certain number of early adolescents is enough to take your minds off being human.

    We have, as a public, given you what no mortals can really absorb without great deterioration of the nervous tract. We have forced you to behave toward beginning adolescents as if they were high school and college kids. We have herded hundreds of these developing bodies into your classrooms. We have ignored the principles of human growth and development that we know are true about junior high children. The "egg carton" theory of education has prevailed even into these latter days, when nearly everyone who knows these youngsters realizes that the last thing they need is to be herded.

You see, dear martyrs, as Mister Dooley once said, "It ain't what I know'd what done me in, it wuz what I know'd that I didn't do nuthin' about." You didn't build the schools; you didn't plan them. You are paid to teach and you do it dutifully, docilely, and with little delinquency. But therein lies some of the trouble. All of us have let someone else do it, even though we know right well that it's bad.

So, let's see what we know, and then let's see what it could mean for teaching this age group.

First, we know that junior high students are very much in the middle of adjusting to biological changes that are sending messages that confuse and hurt them, because they really aren't sure what they mean. Try this one out for size. One clear message is that during these years boys and girls just don't fit together very well. The girls have dreams of glory, while the boys are still dreaming of the days when it was no sweat to be a boy.

So we have pushed the sexes into the same carton, by the hundreds, and we have asked the teachers to try to manage this menagerie of emotions. There is no doubt in the mind of anyone who knows anything about the two sexes that for these years, they are best separated.

Next, at a time when their minds are just starting to grasp the multiple facets of life, the youths have been pushed into identical curriculums with teachers who, for the most part, are devoted to teaching them subject matter, even if it means punishing the students with homework galore, most of which is completely meaningless to the non-devoted scholar.

The junior high school student needs space, a wide

variety of exploratory courses that don't last too long, the opportunity to study and reflect with his own sex, and teachers whose basic commitment is *not* to subject matter. Junior high school students are not little college students. The mass hysteria in this country, in its search for excellence, has led the public to demand scholarship of adolescents that is impossible for them to attain.

Here is an example: Every college professor has seen that, especially with males, the urge to really get down and study often doesn't surface until graduate-school days. Dear teachers, this is not until nearly a decade after the seventh grade!

I have taught hundreds of teachers in the past nineteen years. I can identify a dozen who truly seemed *devoted* to the pursuit of knowledge. Hundreds were good students, but devotion to study was not present in many. Yet, these same folks, particularly those on the secondary levels, demand scholarship from kids who haven't yet settled their identity crisis!

In brief, the junior high school must not be the megalopolis it now is. It should be smaller than the elementary school from which the students came. It should be dispersed on more acreage than are high schools. Its teachers ought to be committed to developing the emotional and social growth of children rather than honing their minds. The teachers and principals should demonstrate about the same knowledge of adolescents that an expert psychiatrist does. Those who fret about the academics of the school ought to teach only in high school.

And so, dear teachers, there it is. Most of what I have said you can't do much about, unless you really want to.

If you do not recognize yourself as fit for the task, may I suggest you bend your energies in other directions. Whoever and wherever you are, you do have the undying thanks of millions in the nation who don't give a hoot what you do; all they care about is that you "only keep the kids in school."

THE CHANGES

Starting a family is change. Living well within a family requires a continual adjustment to change. This part of the book talks about some of the more significant kinds of changes, with the focus especially concerned with adoption, moving, and death.

The latter chapters are especially concerned with a field of study that is becoming more and more openly talked about in America. In the past few years, several books about death have been printed. The most traumatic experience for parents is the death of a child. My concern here is to help those who must suffer through this experience to face it with some greater degree of positive understanding of this most dreadful experience.

Professor John Bowlby of England wrote a multi-volume series called *Psychology of Attachment and Loss* (New York: Basic Books, 1969, 1973). In a sense we may view this series as a study in what happens to children as they grow up in their families, which we call attachment, and what happens as they leave* their families, or loss. All of life is related to our responses to attachment and loss. Most of the changes that occur to people in their family life are either changes of attachment or loss. Learning to cope with these two phenomena constitutes the business of family living. The lives of all children require a great deal of attachment— enough for a child to grow well, to feel secure, and to see himself as wanted and needed. At one and the same time, the family life has to be such that one is able to lose his family or detach from the family and commence his own. Conversely, a family as a unit responds to the loss of any member of that family.

---

*The Bowlby volume on loss does not consider the matter of growing up and leaving the family to start a new one. It does consider what happens to children who are removed from their original families and grow up in institutions or foster situations.

Interfaith marriages

The engaged couple sat silently before me as the impact of what I had just said seemed to settle into their beings. They were the second couple in the past two weeks who, having reached an impasse in their own decision-making processes, sought help from an outside source who might shed light where only darkness seemed to prevail.

"Where the faith of one of the engaged pair is certain and strong and where the religious beliefs of the other are unsure, and if the prospective bride is the one with certain ideals, you may be assured that the children of that marriage will be influenced in the direction of their mother," I said.

I could see that this candid statement hit the young man with a peculiar ferocity. In the last half hour he had said over and over again that he possessed no religious convictions whatever. Indeed, he espoused a finely defined brand of atheism. It had all of the correct pedigrees: he had found that his college experience precluded the possibility of the myths of religion, and his companions had either completely given up the faith of their forefathers or had diluted them to only a fraction of their former selves.

Now marriage and the thought of rearing children of his own had suddenly forced a reappraisal of the realities of his professed disbelief.

Odd, isn't it, how, while one might feel that he has arrived at his absence of religious conviction through the most intellectual of forays, the entire process, once seen as a definitive intellectual decision, becomes somewhat muddied as the thought of passing nothing on to one's children looms large. Should he marry a girl whom he loves but who believes so differently? Rather bemusedly, I thought of how this perennial problem has never been satisfactorily resolved. Wise counselors have always told of the statistics of mixed marriages. But when did statistics ever make any difference to the young? And here a young couple were expecting an answer from one who has only been impressed with the fact that nowhere in the world's history has anyone ever come up with an answer that was satisfactory.

At best, marriage between two persons who have shared the most similar of religious experiences is difficult. While there are always those few couples who spend a lifetime of sharing without ripples of any sort disturbing the union, human experience seems to indicate that even where such a shared religious outlook prevails, there are the usual human difficulties.

Today things aren't what they used to be. Unmarried couples who share the belief that they do not need the dubious benefits of holy matrimony are discovering, according to a report from a New York social work agency, that they are experiencing at least as much difficulty living together as do others. Yet, they share an iconoclasm that should, if anything, bind them together as if by a tight rope. What may be expected from those who join each other with gaping chasms between their cherished ideals?

Simply put, they may expect that in addition to all the usual problems any two humans who decide to marry must face (just because they differ as individuals about everything from toothbrush habits to politics), they will face ideological differences.

Now, it is relatively simple to help couples where overt behavior is obnoxious. They can be taught not to squeeze toothpaste from the middle of the tube. They can be taught to hang up clothes, to brush their teeth before retiring. All of these surface behavioral problems that cause minor difficulties in a marriage can be ameliorated, and they can be changed if one of the two really wants to. But to change a fundamental inside belief, a pervading and guiding feeling that stands at the core of human existence, is virtually impossible.

Of course, one can forget ritual, church, dogma. To do so only requires that the person not do any of the things he did before. On the surface this is entirely possible. But a religious commitment is not necessarily a matter of simply doing certain things. All too often it is feelings that are not easily demonstrable. Thus, change is not a matter of merely ceasing behavior. It has to do with deep-seated emotions, and they are as real as facts and observable behavior.

Finally, a marriage at its best is a coalition. This is not often realized by young folks until they decide to marry. More often it doesn't dawn upon them until their children are growing up. Where mere biology and love are prevalent, many noncoalition activities may be quite successful. Vacations, Christmas, visiting, work schedules, and the like are rather easily amenable to change by one or the other of the partners.

When that first baby comes along, however, things change. A new life brings up memories nearly forgotten in the desire to coexist peaceably. In interfaith marriages, the religious future of the child often becomes paramount, especially if the mother was a devout practitioner prior to marriage. Playing house is over now.

Should people of different faiths marry?

Under the circumstances I have described here, where there is religious commitment of the visceral kind in one or the other, unless there is an absolute agreement about children, the road may be too hazardous to follow.

The family and adoption

Couples usually adopt children because they are unable, for whatever reasons, to have children of their own, and therein lies the source of some of the problems that arise.

If it were only a matter of the couple's adjusting to the fact that they are not able to have children, the problem could be less severe. Most of us, however, live in a world made up of friends, neighbors, brothers, sisters, parents. Usually couples who cannot have children have to face the "slings and arrows" of family and friends who cannot understand what the trouble is.

The incessant chant from the sidelines about when there will be a baby is embarrassing to the couple, guilt producing, and shameful. It is shameful to the couple because they often feel they are letting people down, and it is even more shameful to the family and friends—shameful that they have so little sensitivity to the already complicated emotional life of the young couple.

Friends and relatives should understand that most couples not only want but expect to have children, that there is a great deal of physical and psychological strain placed upon them when they cannot.

Too frequently, people think that a couple's nonfertility has a psychological basis, with the clear implication that perhaps they really don't love one another or really don't want children. This completely mythical belief tests the strength of their relationship as a couple and as individuals. Facing the facts of infertility (I am amazed at how many couples "miraculously" bear children immediately after they adopt a child), if indeed this is a fact, is painful. If a couple can weather that storm, they possess great inner reserves that will help as they decide to adopt.

When a baby is on the way, the parents-to-be receive a great deal of warm and enthusiastic support from everyone who knows and loves them. This acclaim continues with increasing crescendoes as the time of birth approaches.

This is not the case for adoptive parents, who, in fact, receive very little attention except on the day or two following the adoption. Somehow, well-meaning people very quickly ask when they are going to tell the child he is adopted, and then follow this up with the remark that they wonder what it would be like to raise a child not biologically their own.

The implied and often direct emphasis by others that there is a difference between adoptive and natural parents may infuriate the adoptive couple. Indeed, there is a difference, but frequently adoptive parents deny that there is any. Their fury is really a normal reaction to their infertile condition. It would be far better if they could accept their inability to produce children much the same as a diabetic has to admit that he can't have some of those luscious desserts.

There is no reason for feelings of inferiority in either condition. Both are painful. Being unable to have children is probably more so than any other physical problem.

Most often it is the husband who feels the guilt and shame more than his wife. This appears to be wrapped up in a false male machismo. It has no more to do with manhood than the fact of infertility in a female has anything to do with her mothering qualities.

When a couple face the problem together, cry together sufficiently, and then wipe away the tears and proceed to do something about their problem, each is better prepared for adoptive parenthood than most folks are for natural parenthood.

Confronting their life as it is, without blaming and finger pointing, produces the strength they will need to become parents.

After adoption, what?

"The major task in the raising of adopted children is to help them accept the fact that they have had another set of parents." (Group for the Advancement of Psychiatry, *The Joys and Sorrows of Parenthood,* New York: Charles Scribner's Sons, 1973.)

In other words, in addition to every other problem faced by parents as they rear their children, adoptive parents must contend with the shadows of the child's natural parents.

Some folks proclaim in all earnestness that they love their adopted children as their own. I do not doubt this, but that is not the issue here. It is the very real fact that for every adopted child there is some couple, somewhere (be they married or not), who gave birth to that child.

If a child is adopted past the age of two or so, he brings to his new family the images of his original parents. One of the dangers of adopting after this age is that the adoptive parents rarely feel they are the most important persons in the child's life, though it is possible to become very close indeed.

As the child grows older he moves closer to his adoptive parents and the images of childhood's earliest parents fade. For quite some time, though, it is possible for older children to purposely bring up the memories of their first parents so that they can feel a bit sorry for themselves and at the same time increase the ill-at-ease feelings their adoptive parents have had from the first. But soon the child makes a clear distinction between those who birthed him and are not caring for him and those who are providing day-to-day love and sustenance.

Childhood is the process of finding one's identity. The identity crisis becomes acute in adolescence. Thus, the age-old question of when to tell a child that he is adopted comes to the fore. In my opinion, and this is supported by many others, the continual reference to the child's being adopted is unimportant, irrelevant, and too unrelated to his readiness to really comprehend. A natural time to bring up the matter is when he first asks where he came from, and then he can be told.

Experts feel that between seven and ten is about the best time to really delve into the matter of adoption. No matter when the child is told, he may react with frantic reveries about his ideal original parents, and this hurts the adoptive parents. The normal confrontations that occur between parents and their natural children burst into greater fury with adopted ones. It is urgent that these children get all available information during adolescence. If they don't, they may feel the urge to travel and find their parents, which puts further strains upon the family relationship.

As time rolls on, the adopted child accepts his place, stops torturing his adoptive parents, and by the early twenties shows his appreciation for the love and care given him. If parents can survive all this, adoption is a beautiful way to have children when the natural way isn't possible.

Change hurts

A frantic call in the night. "Our daughter left home yesterday and she hasn't come home since." Not too unusual a tale from parents about to move from their home to a nearby state. Their only adolescent daughter, terrified by the thought of losing her peer group and the associations developed over a five-year period, decided to run away and not face the move.

A couple in their early thirties are asked to move almost yearly as the husband climbs the ladder of success in his company. His wife is distraught; she has had it with moving. Their two children, one just in school and the other nearly ready to start, are upset too.

Generally, child-development specialists have felt that if the parents feel good about the move, it is quite likely that their children will accept it more readily. But change is difficult for all humans. It is particularly difficult for adolescents despite their parents' attitudes.

About the most that parents can do with adolescents who will naturally object to any change that tears them away from their peer group is to explain the necessity for change as rationally as possible and indicate that it isn't a matter of choice. Usually, adolescents who are reasonable, able to cope with their surroundings, and have a strong self-image are able to adjust to the thought of the move rather well. In fact, part of their way of "getting even" with their folks is to play the martyr role about the move. Nonetheless, their feelings must be dealt with in a reasoning way, with every indication from their parents that they understand the trauma.

For the most part, the severest time is before the move, since the youngster's imagination creates worlds of problems. Once the move is made, school and social activities usually ensue and all is well again.

It is true, however, that the new student in school during the adolescent years has a hard time cracking the social cliques and alliances that have developed over time. What's more, what is created in the imagination is all imaginary. A sort of self-fulfilling prophecy takes place.

When the new child in school first gets into his new environment, he will avoid any chance for affiliations so that his sense of being the sufferer will, in fact, be fulfilled. After all, he forecasted that he would be miserable; how would it be not to be so? When this wears off, it is natural for most healthy adolescents to seek friends, and thus, while they have preserved their sense of outrage and fulfilled their own prophecies, they are ready to make life liveable again.

In the case of younger children, the change isn't especially consequential because the peer group attachment isn't nearly as strong. Still, when parents are unhappy and apprehensive, their children catch the very same feelings.

Dr. Anna Freud, who worked with children during the blitz in London in World War II, found that when parents accepted the nightly raids better, their children fared better. In fact, she suggested that there are hardly any ordeals children could not survive emotionally if their parents are able to cope.

There is another interesting aspect to the change brought on by moving. Vance Packard and others have noted that, in this age of frequent moves, adults grow further and further away from relatives, longtime friends, and any community bonds unless they are deeply affiliated with religious or social groups that enmesh them no matter where they move. The adults soon adapt an "I don't care" attitude toward their new abode and community and too often find their happiness in instant "palships." These instant associations are too often with others who are transient and uncaring for their community. When the parents' friends are as interchangeable as car parts, you may be sure that their children adopt much the same attitudes.

A mobile life deprives both adults and children of the feeling of belonging. Moving to a community where, for example, there is a cohesive majority further exacerbates the feelings of being left outside, and the "intruders in the dust" retreat further into an uncaring attitude about themselves and their community.

Too often, fathers living under these conditions find their solace in bars and golf courses; mothers may turn to alcohol or nonstop TV watching or may go out to work.

Forty million Americans change their jobs and move every few years. Moving isn't fun. Change can hurt.

Coping with moving

When that moving van pulls up in front of the house, it will very likely be one of "those" days. Some 30 million families move each year, whether they like it or not. The toll upon wives, husbands, and children is more serious than the mere transplanting of tulip bulbs.

One of the objects in life is to develop roots. Although there are always some people suited to the nomadic life, most people need to feel that they belong. One of the powerfully adverse effects of continual moves is the feeling of anomie, or absence of values, that may develop. When people do not feel any affinity for their community, they tend to disregard the laws. Worse than this are the feelings of being outsiders that adults can transmit to children.

Of course, in and of itself it is never bad to know that you are different from the folks who surround you. But there is a difference between knowing that you are unique in a community and feeling that you don't really belong and are, in fact, rejected.

Most rejection, like beauty, lies in the eye of the beholder. When children catch from their parents the feeling of alienation that may accompany a move, they seek out those other children who are similarly alienated. When the parents don't feel that they belong, they often become antisocial and bitter and tend to get their kicks from marginal activities, such as immersing themselves in sports or drink.

One way to survive moving is to consider the place you are moving to not as hostile territory, but rather as a laboratory where it will be possible for you to learn.

Back in World War II when I was seventeen and had enlisted in the Aviation Cadets of the United States Air Force, I was under the distinct impression that anyone who came from some place other than New York City must necessarily be a backward, illiterate hick. Imagine my chagrin when I, through some fortuitous circumstances that appeared to be disastrous then, was transferred from my unit to a new group from Iowa. I was really in for a case of culture shock. I learned in no time that these folks had feelings, intelligence, even culture!

When people move, they owe it to their children not to predispose them toward feeling alien. On the other hand, I am not necessarily advocating that children be told they may not differ from their neighbors. I am saying, however, that it is not wise for parents to set barriers to their children's happiness by heightening their feelings of difference.

It is tough enough for children to move into their new surroundings without feelings of trepidation. It is even more traumatic to try to break into a new group when parents have warned their children of the evils of that group. Instead, it is important that parents seek the strengths of their new community and affiliate with its drives toward producing a better life. When new folks at least try to join in the efforts of communities to enhance their life-style, the older residents will sense this good will and reciprocate.

Adults should never, for themselves and the good of their children, walk about with the proverbial "chip on the shoulder," almost daring everyone around them to knock it off. That chip will soon transfer to their children.

Adults can get away from it all in a number of ways. If the world is too much with them, they can take off for a weekend somewhere; but children are stuck with no means of escaping from their alienation, boredom, or even disgust. They just have to face it day in, day out. Should it really get to them too much, they learn how to find others who are unhappy, and thus they begin associations with others in the peer group who have learned to hate. When children hate, they rebel and indulge in activities they would never have countenanced before. Alienation is the precursor to aberrant social activity.

Coping with moving does not mean capitulation to the norms of the new neighborhood. It does mean accommodation, understanding, and the transmittal of this attitude to children. Moving hurts less when children enter their new territory with good feelings and a sense of adventure rather than disaster.

When a little child is dying

The death or imminent death of a child is one of life's great tragedies. In the opinion of many who have studied the reactions to death of preschool-age children, it is far worse for the parents than for the child himself. No more difficult question is asked of parents than when a three-year-old asks if he is going to die. When all of the medical evidence indicates there is no hope, the fact of death must be faced squarely. If the child asks such a question, the only answer is, "Yes, all of us die some day, and you too will die, but not right now."

The preschool child can face his own dying only with very rudimentary, even primitive understanding, and with limited emotional strength. The most difficult thing for the toddler facing death is to see the adults around him overcome with grief.

It is imperative that mothers and fathers, even at the risk of putting on a false front, not show absolute despair. The young child has learned to understand death; he has not learned to react to dying.

Kornei Chukovsky, a great Russian poet and storyteller,

in his book *From Two to Five* (University of California Press) tells of a preschooler in Russia who asked her grandmother quite matter-of-factly when the elderly lady was going to die. To the grandmother's reply of "Soon," the child replied, "Good, then I can have your eyeglasses, Granny."

There is no irreverence here, at least on the part of a three-year-old. Death is virtually meaningless in terms of its real relationship to him.

Even if the child has had numerous nonhuman experiences with death, such as the death of a turtle, canary, or a porcupine along the road, these were things with a nonpersonal relationship to him.

The preschool-age child is in the process of evolving independence of thought and judgment. Thus, when he is faced with the imminence of his own death, he is almost totally dependent upon the adults around him for guidelines about how to react. His personal dying has meaning only in terms of the grown-ups he knows best—usually his mother and father. If they appear distraught (they usually are), then he begins to panic and becomes similarly distracted about his position.

Hospitalization is more traumatic to the dying preschooler than the fact of his imminent demise. In the hospital he is suddenly faced with some very tangible facts; he is not at home, and he responds to this totally. He yearns for a familiar face. Whenever a face does appear, it usually means he will be hurt by a needle or a laboratory test. When a child under the age of three is hospitalized, he needs his mother or a reasonable facsimile. It is extremely important that hospitals realize this and provide the necessary freedom so that parents don't feel guilty about visiting, staying all night or all day, and in general being omnipresent. Wise hospital administrators learn to use the help of mother as part of the treatment. A mother can provide the bridge between fear and security, thus making medication, surgery, and pain-killing a less arduous nursing task.

One interesting facet of the young child's hospitalization is the fact that he feels a great deal of anger at being hospitalized. First, he is at the developmental stage where he is beginning to separate himself a bit from his parents and to have his own ideas and thoughts. Since people and things are seen in terms of black or white, good or bad, he finds that his bad thoughts and ideas are directed against people and things with which he interacts daily.

There is, for the child at this age, much interest in exploring, finding out, doing bad things for which he often gets punished. Finding himself suddenly in the hospital seems to be punishment for something that he has done or thought in the past. This inner fear builds up so that he starts to treat patients and staff at hospital with a great deal of hostility. He is overburdened with anger, guilt, and loneliness, and it is expected that he will be sassy and brash. If hospital personnel don't understand this, they punish him further.

As he grows older, nearer four and five, he develops more knowledge about death and the realization of it. Though he may appear unconcerned, it is gnawing at his innards, and his play may start to be about funerals, coffins, and the deaths of others. This is his way of working out his own misery. He will start to try to explain this awesome phenomenon for himself. If he asks about his illness, the answers should be precise and to the point and should tell no more than his questions ask. Even to the very direct question "Will I die?" the answer should be direct, true, and implicate all people.

Five-year-olds may be comforted finally by being told that death means sleeping in the arms of God. For the child whose religious experience has a definite explanation for death, there is some extra comfort in believing that not only will he be with his Maker, but that he will also eventually be joined by his entire family. At this point his parents can openly say that they will be sad, that they love him very, very much, and that his death is not a sending away because of any badness.

The experience of death for the preschooler will, at best, be painful. Indeed, it will be more so to his parents and family. The temporary nature of the separation can be healing to all. To those whose religious feelings do not allow for this last bit of comfort, it is suggested that at least the sleep symbol might be the lesser dread. Except in the case of dyed-in-the-wool atheists, the analogy of God and his loving arms might make the dying child's end easier.

The dying child is a tragic sight. His management until the end can be made more decent if parents and hospitals would understand a bit more of the psychology of death to one so young.

When a child is dying— a trauma for loved ones

Invariably, parents who are told of the fatal illness of their child react with disbelief. They frequently say they do not believe it and will not accept it. Often they will start a frantic round of taking the child from clinic to clinic here, there, and everywhere.

To prevent their embarrassment, wise doctors will immediately suggest second and third medical opinions. It is important that parents do not start the endless round of consultations, which often end with quacks, because this only builds feelings of denial that must soon give way to accepting and learning to cope with the tragic news.

These cold words cannot convey the dread that must grip the hearts of these parents, the panic that must energize their desire to move heaven and earth to stay the execution of medical judgment. Yet, the truth must be faced, hysteria must be curbed, and all of the family must turn and face the imminent loss. In this process they will find sadness, physical exhaustion, and irritability. This they must somehow learn to encounter in each other with patience, love, and sweet understanding. They will also find in themselves deeper feelings of self-worth as they begin to plumb the depths of their own emotional capacities.

The entire family will suffer. They will often begin to become angry not only at themselves and each other but also at the dying child. After all, despite the fact that he had no hand in this, he is the cause of a great deal of family upset. The contemplation of the dying child's leaving them may make parents angry enough to attack each other. Brothers and sisters in the family may begin to pick at one another—all of this apparent disintegration because they care so deeply and are grieving so wholeheartedly for the dying child.

Self-blame becomes a very threatening fact of life. Parents may feel that they have been at fault for not paying closer attention, for remarks made in past years that were unkind, for not feeding the child better. Brothers and sisters, too, may feel that they have not been adequate. Should the child be old enough to sense these self-hatred types of feelings, then he begins to assume the burden that is not even rightfully that of his parents, his brothers, or his sisters.

During the time that a child is dying there is, unlike when death is sudden, time for the family to adjust to death. It is a time when the family must learn how to reinvest itself emotionally. This is the time for the family to change its goals and plans, to channel their mourning anger in a productive way. It is too simple to attack oneself for what was surely no fault. It is too cruel to turn on physicians and hospitals who played no part in the tragedy. I have known families who, at this time, have even lost their religious faith—blaming God for this unjust act.

It is possible for parents and siblings to turn to activities in the community, such as cystic fibrosis or leukemia organizations, so that through the death of one family's child the lives of others may one day be saved.

When a child is turned over to a hospital for treatment, both he and his parents quite rightfully feel that they have lost control of the situation. In a very real sense this is true. Once the child is removed from home, the locus of control is with the medical authorities. The child, feeling this helplessness, may make his own parents the victims of his fear. He may taunt them for their ineffectiveness, cruel as it may seem. And once at the hospital the parents have an "out" also. It is possible that they may feel a great sense of relief and start to imagine that the medical people will come up with a miracle. When this is not forthcoming, then physicians may become the brunt of family aggression.

When children are dying over a protracted period of time, it is natural for the family to reinvest time with other people, other children, and other activities during this process. Inevitably they turn from the child who is dying in order to survive the ordeal they have been through. If he has not yet died, this is very difficult for the child who senses this emotional detachment. It is urgent for all concerned that the withdrawal, which is mourning, be not accomplished too soon, for then the child dies alone and unwanted even though he is surrounded by loved ones.

One last point: the Lazarus syndrome as identified in William Easson's *The Dying Child* (Springfield: Charles C. Thomas, 1970) occurs when a child has had a remission or indeed a recovery, so that he now needs to reenter the family after they have emotionally left him and come to terms with the imminence of his death. He is, as it were, reborn into the family, and everyone needs to readjust based upon this new happening.

Mourning for mates

As we grow older, we are faced more frequently with the death of adults we know or love. More often we need to deal with those left after death—the mourners, particularly widows (they constitute the largest share of the adult bereaved), who need somehow to reconstruct their lives and endure to the end.

Those who have studied adult bereavement recognize four fairly distinct phases adults go through as they attempt finally to adjust to the loss of, for example, a husband. These are:

1. Numbness
2. Yearning and searching
3. Disorganization and despair
4. Greater or lesser degree of reorganization

Let's examine each of these phases:

1. *Numbness.* Studies of widows, especially younger women, seem to indicate that most, when told of their husbands' deaths, were stunned. Some said they "felt nothing at all." Many widows reported that the news failed to even register at first. This first phase lasts from a few hours to a

week and is often interrupted by outbursts of extreme emotion, usually crying uncontrollably. These outbursts are based upon fear, often anger, and, on occasion, elation. Obviously the last emotion is not a genuine reaction to death, but a peculiar manifestation of extreme agitation that surfaces as elation.

2. *Yearning and searching.* When the reality of her loss starts to dawn on the widow, she normally becomes restless and preoccupied with thoughts of the deceased. These thoughts are often accompanied by a sense of the deceased actually being present on occasion. Even sounds once familiar (such as the turning of the door handle at about 5:30 P.M.) may be momentarily interpreted as the husband returning from work as he had always done.

Concomitant with this yearning behavior is a very odd reaction, especially from usually rational and intelligent people who are experiencing the pains of mourning—the searching behavior. It isn't uncommon for sane adults to follow down the street or through a store persons who, at first glance, appear to bear a strong resemblance to the deceased.

3. *Disorganization and despair.* It may appear strange, even somewhat incredulous, that mourning behavior often includes anger. Indeed, for the widow to be angry—at herself, her husband, her doctor, clergyman, even children—is not a sign of a sick person or one who is incapable of facing reality.

Studies have shown that many widows, especially in the early days of their bereavement, feel anger. To hold oneself or friends, even the deceased husband, responsible ("Why did he leave me alone?") is also normal. Anger and reproach, while normal, are part of the despair reaction to being "deserted." One phenomenon that accompanies anger is really the beginning of entering the fourth phase, reorganization.

4. *Reorganization.* This is the often sudden attachment a widow may develop toward someone who is seen as a steady symbol. This may be, and often is, some relative, an employer, an older person in the community. There is no shame in this reaction. Attachment behavior, too often called dependence, is a positive step in readjustment. Too often in our society dependence has a negative connotation. Criticism of widows who demonstrate attachment behavior is unfair and cruel. It is a sign of beginning recovery.

Researchers indicate that most women, especially younger ones, take more than a year to really become themselves again. One study showed that after a year, 20 percent of widows were still in poor health, in a disturbed emotional state, usually not entering into any strong reorganizational type of behavior.

The human and natural response to death is and must be mourning. It cannot and should not be avoided.

Helping those who mourn

A young widow recently complained that immediately after the death of her husband, even her closest friends and relatives seemed to be bound in a conspiracy of silence. There are healthy conditions for mourning and unhealthy ones. The most valuable experience in a healthy bereavement is for the person in mourning to be able to express his feelings. "Give sorrow words," wrote Shakespeare. "The grief that does not speak knits up the o'erwrought heart and bids it break."

For those who surround the mourning widow, and for the bereaved herself, the difficult question is how—how to help the survivor talk of death, how to listen to that person's feelings. When it is understood that the most disturbing effects aroused by the loss are fear of being abandoned, yearning for the lost figure, and anger that he cannot be found, both the bereaved and his close friends and kin may start to appreciate their respective roles. Whether an adult or a child is mourning, the assistance of a trusted person is indispensable if he is to recover from the loss.

Those who have seriously researched the process of

mourning contend that the bereaved person is, especially in the first year of his loss, struggling with the past. Happier days have been taken away. The remaining person in a marriage, for example, is searching for some way to turn away from the reality of death and to recapture a happier past.

How can those who live with the mourner help to release the flood of emotion so often dammed up?

First, we must see his world from his point of view. His feelings are facts even though he may regard his behavior and attitude as being totally unrealistic. For instance, a middle-aged widow refused to move or redecorate her apartment. All of her friends felt she needed this lift—sort of like buying a new hat or dress when you have the blahs. But this woman expected her husband to one day soon walk in the door. She *knew* the hospital had make a mistake. To argue with the unreality of her reasoning would be unproductive. Her desire to have the place be just as he left it is a very real part of her grief pattern.

The grieving person must be able to express hurt and sorrow. He is less likely to do so to folks who don't respect his feelings no matter how unrealistic they are or seem to be. The role of a true friend is clearly one of supporter even for odd behavior. After all, unless there has been a visible and complete mental collapse (and this is very rare) the grieving person knows that his world has changed. Yet, he wants not to let go. This is normal and natural. Those who verbally or nonverbally show disdain for the manifestations of grief in the bereaved cannot help "give sorrow words."

It takes time to reconcile oneself to the reality of loss, and the temporary unrealism needs to be understood. Sympathy for the obviously unreal solution to the problem of grief is a necessity. Thus, the good friend needs to say, "Well, you know, it may be a good idea not to change things for a while. You'll feel more comfortable with the old paint and drapes. Why not do what you feel you need to. Hurting out loud helps, and I'll listen if you need me to."

Chronic grief over more than a year's period of time usually results from the person's overattachment to the lost spouse, the lack of a close relationship with another member of the family, and the absence of any interests to distract him from his grief.

There is often an element of self-punishment too. Ordinarily, psychotherapeutic help can be of some use. Most important is the continued sympathy and love of family, the help of clergy, and the friendship of others in a similar position.

Expressing the hope that a person will "pull himself together" is hurtful advice. A study of grieving widows indicated that if, after a year, their condition was unfavorable, they reported that they received too little encouragement to express their grief and anger or to talk about their dead husbands and the past they once shared.

Widows who did well with their grief said that the people they contacted made it easy for them to express the intensity of their feelings.

EPILOGUE

I spent last night with dear parents, who today celebrated fifty years of marriage. We spent some all too short hours talking of my childhood, their marriage, my only sibling, a sister. I'm well aware of Thoreau's admonition that the old have, in fact, nothing to teach the young. Perhaps he meant that the young never listen to what the old have to teach. He may even have meant that the reflections of the elderly never accurately mirror the years that have passed. It has been said that when one looks at the past, he does so with more than a passing forgetfulness of everything that hurts. So be it.

My parents met when both were very young. My mother was orphaned at thirteen, and the five children were raised in an orphanage until, one by one, some kind of shelter was found for them. Mother was sent to live with an eighty-year-old lady who didn't speak English.

Dad lived just across the street with his five brothers and sisters. His parents were the janitors of an apartment house, and neither spoke English; in fact, neither had learned it even at the time of their deaths thirty years later.

When my father first set eyes upon my mother, he was so startled by her beauty and so conscious of his own "homeliness" (at sixteen that's how he saw himself) that he dared look upon her only by the devious means of poking a hole through the center of a newspaper and devouring the sight completely unknown to her. The watchful waiting ended with the "scrawny beast" begging for her hand. She had no one to consult with but an old lady who couldn't have cared less what her charge did. And so they were married. It wasn't very long before I came along, followed soon after by my sister.

Of the ten children who had been born to my grandparents, only one was graduated from college. Most went to high school; some finished. Of the eight children born to those ten children, six graduated from colleges, two with doctor's degrees. This brings us to that fiftieth anniversary celebration and what we learned from Nana and Papa Landau.

We learned that in half a century neither of them had changed the other—not one bit. I have heard my mother lament through the years that my dad played too much tennis for his age, and on the day of their fiftieth year of marriage he and I played four sets of doubles, and he won two of the four. During that same period of time I heard Dad complain only that Mother inhibited his tennis-playing activities. In four days of festivities we heard very little of the bad times or of petty annoyances.

On the evening of their anniversary, Father slipped a delicate gold ring on mother's wedding finger. He had made it himself, and in about ¼-inch high letters that encircled the ring, he had laboriously carved "50 YEARS OF LOVE."

Mother's words to the young and old who gathered for the formal party were, "To separate would have been easy; to stay together was difficult but worth it."

A grandchild "saw" the marriage this way as she wrote in the historical scrapbook gathered for the occasion: "Nana Bee and Papa Herman are like a peanut butter sandwich —all stuck together."

Index

A

Absolutism in communication, 99
Addiction, causes of, 43, 70-73, 77-79; family-related problems of, 74
Adolescence, length of, 5; development during, 28-29; problems in, 66-67; and drugs, 77-79; communication during, 98-100; youths in trouble during, 114-15; behavior during, 172-75; definition of, 172-73; religious revolt during, 193-95; problems in junior high school during, 196-99
Adoption, 141-42, 207-209, 210-12
Adult bereavement, 227-29
Adulthood, mark of, 177

Agee, James, 2
Aggressiveness in children, 5, 52
Alcoholism, effect of on children, 55, 72
Altruistic behavior, 131
American family, 4-9
American Family, The, 49-50
American Orthopsychiatric Association, 30
Antisocial behavior, signs of, 51-52
Approval, ways to express, 125-26
Assertive women, 8
Authoritarian parent, 116
Authoritative parent, 117
Authority models, 5-6
Aviation Cadets, experience in, 217

B

Baden, Michael, 80

Baumrind, Dr. Diane, 118
Behavior modification, 88; how children learn, 89; changing, 89-90; learned, 94; results of good, 125-26; positive, 127-29; praising, in children, 130-31
Bell, T. H., 160
Bereavement, effects of, 227-29
Bowlby, John, 201
Boys, sex education for, 179-82
Break-up, family, 48-49
Brill, Leon, 43, 74, 75
British mother and author, comment of, 5
Bruch, Hilda, 61-63

C

Categories or types of children, 149-51
Changing times, 168-71
Chess, Stella, 149
Child Development: A Core Approach, 157
Child in the Family, The, 61-62
Childhood and Society, 117, 175
Children, learning needs of, 12; not responsible for parents' happiness, 17-18; responses of, in wartime, 19-20; inner strengths of, 21; growth processes of, 23-26; delinquent behavior in, 41-44; differences of, in school, 51-53; learn hostility at home, 54-55; independence of, 144; growth patterns of, 146-48; three types of, 149-51; easy, 149-50; difficult, 150-51; slow-to-warm-up, 151; basic needs of, 152-54; learning difficulties of, 155; competition among, 161-64; teaching honesty to, 190-91; religion and, 193-94; of interfaith marriages, 203-206; dying, 219-22, 223-26
Chukovsky, Kornei, 219
Clark, Kenneth, 130
Cloisters in New York City, 1
Coalition in families, 16
Columbia University, 61
Communal marriage, 177
Communes, 11
Communication in families, 14, 94-97, 98-100, 101-103
Community life of family, 136-38
Competition among children, 161-64
Conjoint Family Therapy, 122
Covert signals in communication, 103

Creative Parent-Teacher Conferences, 42
Cuddling children, 102

D

Day-care centers, 30
De-Addiction Process, 43, 74, 75
Death, of child, 219-22, 223-26; of spouse, 227-29
Death in the Family, A, 2
Death of a Salesman, 48
Delinquent behavior in children, 41-44
Della-Piana, Gabriel, 159
Developmental stages of growth, 155-57
Dictionary for the Disenchanted, 30
Diet, importance of, 159
Direction without dictation, 115
Division of Family Services of Utah, 107
Divorce statistics, 10; effect of, on children, 55; and drug addiction, 74-75
Double-bind message, 52-53
Drugs, youth on, 46, 68, 70-73, 80-82; therapy, 84
Dying Child, The, 225

E

Easson, William, 225

Eating and obesity, 58-59
Education in the home, 160
Educational Alliance, 65
Ego-identity crisis, 177
Emotional divorce, 74-75
Emotional involvement in families, 14
Emulsion, family is like, 3
England, child in residential center in, 36-38
Equality of children in family, 5
Erikson, Erik, 117, 152-53, 175, 176
Esalen, 104
Ethics, teaching, 8
Evolution of families, 23-26
Extended families, 12
Eye-level communication, 97.

F

Family, is more than sum of parts, 1-3; tapestry of, 1-2; in America today, 4-9; is not obsolete, 10-12; avoiding failure in, 12; biology of, 13-15; generations in, 13; emotional involvement in, 14; function of, in developing children, 16-18; disintegration of, 16; evolution of, 23-26; goal-oriented, 42-43; life of, is not

tranquil, 45-46; break-ups of, 48-49; effects of, on child in school, 54-56; of drug addict, 74-76; therapy, 91; is social system, 111; needs rules, 111-13; values taught in, 114-15; discipline in, 116-18; traditions, 133-35; community life of, 136-38; purpose of, 141-45; responsibilities of, to each member, 142-43; interactions of members of, 143-44
Family Interaction Grid, 88, 107-110
Family Services of Utah, Division of, 107
Fat children, 57-60, 61-64
Fathers, responsibilities of, 43-44, 179-82
Feeding, problems of children, 24-25; patterns of children, 147-48
Fiddler on the Roof, 133
Firmness in families, 114
Fish brain food, 158
Flower children, 65
Fondling, 104-106
Food and Drug Administration, 71
Foster care, 36-38
Freedom for children, 119-21

Freedom—Not License, 119-20
Freud, Anna, 19, 172, 173, 215
Freud, Sigmund, 43, 152
Friedman, Robert, 41
From Two to Five, 220
Frost, Robert, 21

G

Gas station, incident in, 190-92
German father, 117
Gender-linked roles, 18
Generations in family life, 13, 14, 16-17
Gibson, William, 2
Ginott, Haim, 88
Glueck, Sheldon and Eleanor, 41, 74
Goal-oriented family life, 42
Gordon's methodology, 88
Group for the Advancement of Psychiatry, 194, 210
Growth process of children, 22-26

H

Happiness, quest for, 83-85
Harlow, Harry, 104-105
Home, parent-child relationships in, 44; as therapeutic community, 88
Hospitalization, effect of, on child, 220-21

How to Talk With Children, 159

I

Identity, adolescent struggle for, 174, 176-78; adopted child's search for, 211
Illinois Drug Abuse programs, 72
Independence of children, 6, 144-45
Individual's Commitment Plan, 109
Individuality of family member, 137
Infantalism of youth, 168-71
Infants, dependency of, 23; needs of, 27
Inner strengths of children, 21-22
Interfaith marriage, 203-206
Israeli kibbutz, 32, 137

J

Japan, suicides in, 163
Jefferson, Thomas, 165
John (film), 36-38
Joys and Sorrows of Parenthood, 194, 210
Julius Caesar, 61
Junior high school, problems in, 196-99

K

Kagan, Jerome, 131, 157

Kibbutz, Israeli, 32, 137
Kindness, giving praise for, 130-32
Knight, James A., 114

L

Lane, Howard, 41, 88, 168
Lazarus syndrome, 225
Learned behavior, 94
Learning difficulties, 155
Lee, Richard V., 184
License and freedom in discipline, 119-21
Lidz, Theodore, 11
L'il Abner, 31
Linkage to institutions, 136-38
Listening in families, 94-97; to adolescents, 98-100; with third ear, 101-103
Little Prince, The, 133
London blitz, children in, 19-20, 215
Loud family, on television series, 49-50
Love, marrying for, 4; need of children for, 21; definitions of, 31-32; in teenagers, 187-89

M

Male authority, erosion of, 7
Malnourished Mind, The, 156
Marasmus, 105

Marijuana, dangers of, 77-79
Marriage, merging backgrounds in, 13-14; sex before, 183-86; interfaith, 203-206
Mate selection in America, 5, 6
Maturity in families, 15
Mass for the Dead, A, 2
McKay, David O., 21, 167
Mead, Margaret, 38
Message, double-bind, 52-53
Methadone, 71, 81
Military experience of author, 217
Mobility of today's family, 213-15
Money, effect of, on character development, 165-67
Monkeys, experiment with, 104-105
Mother, guilt patterns in, 43; who won't let go of children, 55-56; effect of, on obese child, 61-64; and drug addiction, 74-75; overprotective, 75; substitutes for, 153
Mothercraft, 33-35
Motherhood, anxieties of, 7-8
Mothers-in-law, living with, 35
Mourning, 230-32

Movie ratings, 184
Moving, effects on family of, 213-15, 216-18
Multi-generational families, 33-35
Music lessons, 125-26

N

Needs of children, 152-54
Neill, A. S., 119-20
New York City, teaching in slums of, 43; youth who dies of drug overdose in, 80-82
New York *Times,* articles in, 130-31, 184
Nonconformity in school, 54

O

Obesity, 57-60, 61-64
Odyssey House, 72-73, 78, 80
Outside institutions, 136-38

P

Pacing of individual child, 148
Parent-teacher conferences, 42
Parental Authority Research Project, 118
Parents, coalition of, 17; development of, 27-29; preparation of, 46-47; and discipline, 116-18; of author, 235-37

Peer group, importance of, 25, 28, 75
People Making, 122
Permissive parent, 118
Person, The, 11
Phobia, school, 55, 56
Pills, adults taking, 70-71
Poland, rabbi in, 91
Porcupines, story about, 10
Positive behavior, encouraging, 127-29
Preschoolers, 28, 158-60
Prisoners of war, 105, 134
Professional's Intervention Plan, 109
Promiscuity, sexual, 186
Psychology of Attachment and Love, 201

R

Religion in families, 193-95, 203-206
Repressiveness at home, 52-53
Rogerian analysis, 88
Rosenberg, Bernard, 30
Rules needed in families, 111-13
Rural life, 169, 170
Russell, Bertrand, 130-31
Russia, family life in, 8, 11

S

San Francisco, flower children in, 65
San Francisco State University, 41
Satir, Virginia, 122
Schizophrenia in children, 90
Schneouer, Elie, 155
Scholastic grades, 131-32
School, trauma of failure in, 20-21; difficulties of children in, 51-56; nonconformity in, 54; phobia, 55-56
Schopenhauer, 10
Seeking, growth pattern of child, 146-47
Self-esteem, need for, 122-24
Self-selection of children, 149
Senay, Edward, 72
Sex, roles, 18; before marriage, 183; education for boys, 179-82
Sibling competition, 161
Soap operas on television, 91, 92
St. Exupéry, Antoine de, 133
Standards in family, 190-92
Stepchildren, rearing, 107-110
"Street people," 65-69
Summerhill, 119
Symbiotic relationship, 24, 75

T

Television series on American

family, 49-50; influence of, 91, 92
Tennis, competition in, 162-63
Therapy, family, 91
Third ear, listening with, 101-103
Time magazine, article on drug addiction in, 71
Toddlerhood, 27-28
Touching in communication, 104-106
Traditions in families, 133-35
Trauma of children in wartime, 20, 215

U

University of Southern California Gerontology Center, 156
Upper respiratory infections, 34

V

Value systems in children, 131-32

Values, teaching, 12, 190-92
Van de Velde, 184
Virginity, 183-86

W

Wartime, children in, 19-20, 215
White, Burton, 157, 159
Widows, 227-32
Wiley, Philip, 43
Women, decision-making authority of, 7; assertive, 8; working, 17; some unsuited for motherhood, 31
Women's liberation movement, 43
Working mothers, 17, 34-35

Y

You and Your Child's World, 161
Young Children in Wartime, 19
Your Child's Intellect, 160